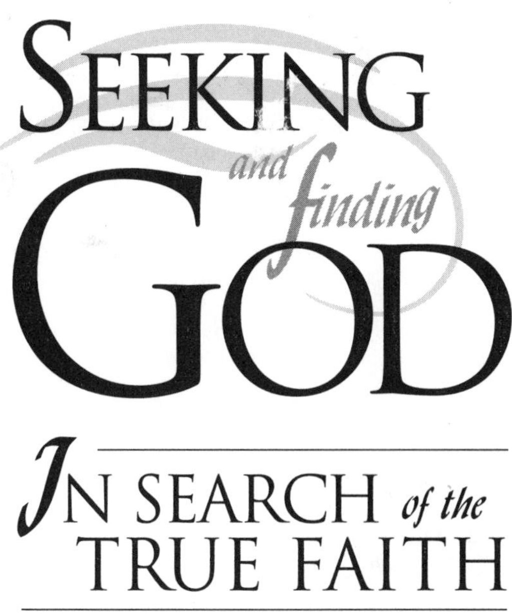

SEEKING and finding GOD

IN SEARCH of the TRUE FAITH

DAVE HUNT

BEND • OREGON

Except where otherwise indicated, all Scripture quotations in this book are taken from the King James Version of the Bible.

Verses marked NASB are taken from the New American Standard Bible®, ©1960,1962,1963,1968,1971,1972,1973,1975,1977, 1995 by The Lockman Foundation. Used by permission.

Italics used in Scripture references are added for emphasis by the author.

First Printing July 2004
Second Printing April 2005 (revised & expanded)

The author's free monthly newsletter, THE BEREAN CALL, *may be received by sending a request to the address below, or by calling 1-800-937-6638.*
To register for free e-mail updates, to access our digital archive and to purchase resource materials online, visit us at: www.thebereancall.org

SEEKING AND FINDING GOD

Published by The Berean Call
PO Box 7019, Bend, OR 97708

Second Edition ISBN: 1-928660-23-1
(First Edition ISBN: 1-928660-14-2)

Library of Congress Control Number: 2005923634

Some material for this volume is derived from *An Urgent Call to a Serious Faith* by Dave Hunt (The Berean Call, ISBN: 1-928660-06-1, previously published by Harvest House Publishers, ISBN: 0-7369-0313-5)

Printed in the United States of America

Contents

And ye shall seek me, and find me,
when ye shall search for me
with all your heart.

—JEREMIAH 29:13

1

The Necessity *of* Certainty

Teach us to number our days, that we may apply our hearts unto wisdom.

—Psalm 90:12

Death is not a pleasant topic, nor one that we will dwell upon, but it is an important starting point for serious reflection. Moses wrote, "So teach us to number our days [that is, to realize how quickly they come to an end], that we may apply our hearts unto wisdom" (Psalm 90:12). The implication is clear that something lies beyond the grave for which we ought to make plans. In full agreement, King David wrote, "Lord, make me to know mine end...the measure of my days...that I may know how frail I am" (Psalm 39:4). That realization would only be depressing and much to be avoided unless there is something (good or bad) after death for which we should prepare. In the same vein, Solomon declared: "It is better to go to the house of mourning [that is, a funeral], than to go to the house of feasting: for that is the end of all men; and the living will lay it to his heart" (Ecclesiastes 7:2).

THE NECESSITY OF ABSOLUTE CERTAINTY

The uncertainty of life and the inevitability of death are two of the most basic elements of human existence. Logically, then—even for those who think death ends it all—what *may* lie after death deserves at least some serious attention and planning before it may be forever too late. And it is only reasonable that prior to that awesome moment of death, which overtakes all in its own time and without discrimination, one needs to be absolutely certain of what death will bring and exactly why.

Absolutely certain? Of course, because nothing less will do. Regardless of one's religious belief or lack of it, death puts its terminating stamp upon every earthly passion, position, possession, and ambition. There is a finality to death that shouts, "Too late! Too late!"

Inasmuch as death could come knocking at any time, regardless of one's age, health, or expectations, there is great urgency in knowing—with certainty beyond question—what lies beyond death's door. No matter how young we may be or how healthy we may seem, that dread event draws steadily and inexorably closer for each one of us—and often comes as an unwelcome surprise.

THE CERTAINTY AND CHALLENGE OF DEATH

Of Juliet, Lady Capulet mourned, "Death lies on her like an untimely frost upon the sweetest flower of the field." In *Paradise Lost,* Milton expressed the universal horror that anyone could become "Food for so foul a Monster" as death. Homer's *Iliad,* written in the eighth century B.C., lamented, "Death in ten thousand shapes hangs ever over our heads, and no man can elude him." That being the case, there is great urgency to know what lies before us when death releases us from these material bodies. There is no known recovery once one passes through death's door into whatever lies beyond.

Inasmuch as death could come knocking at any time...there is great urgency in knowing—with certainty beyond question—what lies beyond death's door.

The view that death's consequences ought to be a matter of grave concern is opposed by three alternative beliefs. Some insist that there is nothing beyond death either to prepare for or to fear. Their mantra, which they desperately want to believe in order to be relieved of any thought of possible judgment, goes like this: "When you're dead, you're dead; that's it, period."

Others, while believing in an afterlife, still manage to relieve themselves of any concern by subscribing to the theory that in the next life our spirits meet perfect acceptance no matter what we may have done in this life. We simply continue to learn further lessons as we progress ever upward.

Still others are convinced that our souls migrate into new bodies, providing the opportunity to come back to earth to live again and again, hopefully to progress in each succeeding life.

When You're Dead, You're Dead—Or Are You?

We'll consider these three popular theories, the first one in this chapter and the other two in the next. The idea that death is the end of one's existence is founded upon materialism: the theory that nothing exists but matter. Therefore, there is no soul or spirit to survive the death of the body; nor do God, Satan, angels, devils, or anything else that isn't physical exist. This atheistic theory is appealing, and many would like to believe it because there would be no future judgment to face for one's misdeeds. Such a belief can be easily dismissed, however, on the basis of much evidence to the contrary.

One of the major products of materialism is the theory of evolution (which we will consider later). If all we are is the material of our bodies, then evolution might have some validity. But if there is a nonphysical part of man that animals don't have (for which there is abundant proof), then evolution of the physical body could never explain the development of humans. Furthermore, that difference would constitute an impassable chasm preventing any evolutionary ancestral relationship between animals and man. This was pointed out clearly by Mortimer J. Adler, Chicago University philosophy professor, co-founder of the *Great Books of the Western World*, and an editor of the *Encyclopedia Britannica*, in his important 1967 book, *The Difference of Man and the Difference it Makes*.

To the ancient assertion, "I think, therefore I am," must be added, "My thoughts are nonmaterial; therefore, so am I."

That we are each more than our physical bodies is evident from the fact that we hold ideas and thoughts that are not physical and therefore cannot be part of the physical brain. Our thoughts are not the result of stimuli from the physical world around us. A common misconception is the idea that we think in pictures: in our mind we see a cow, or a tree, or a car, etc. But this last sentence has a number of words for which there is no physical object to picture. What is the picture of "common," or "misconception," or "idea," or "think," or "mind"?

To the ancient assertion, "I think, therefore I am," must be added, "My thoughts are nonmaterial; therefore, so am I." That being the case, where do these thoughts reside, what form do they take, and what is their origin? These questions, for which materialism has no answer, must be seriously and honestly faced if we are to understand ourselves.

More than Matter

There is no way that chemical reactions and electrical impulses among the brain's cells can explain a sense of right and wrong, the beauty of a sunset, or the rational and moral choices we continually make. No material of any kind, either in the brain or outside of it, has any qualities to explain our ability to understand ideas such as truth, justice, holiness, mercy, and grace. These concepts are totally nonphysical. They do not originate within the brain, nor are they a conditioned response to anything anywhere in the entire physical universe.

If thoughts originated in the brain, we would be prisoners of our brains, wondering what our brain would think of next...

Indeed, the brain does not conceive creative ideas or originate thoughts. If thoughts originated in the brain, we would be prisoners of our brains, wondering what our brain would think of next and compelled to do whatever the brain decided. On the contrary, every person is convinced that he or she makes rational choices by weighing alternatives, not because the brain gets an impulse to make the body act in a certain way. While we are *prone* to react impulsively to the stimuli of physical temptations that breed desires, we are not *forced* to do so. The moral struggles we all experience to resist temptation are proof that we are not stimulus-response mechanisms ruled by impulses but that we do make genuine choices, though our choices are not always rational or morally right.

Without a doubt, there is a "ghost in the machine"—something nonphysical inhabiting the body. There must be a human spirit, which thinks these nonphysical thoughts, holds these concepts that have no source in the physical universe, and makes rational and moral choices—or irrational and immoral ones. The brain is like a computer, which the spirit (the thinking, choosing person within) uses to operate the body in order to function in this physical universe of space, time, and matter—and to interact with other souls and spirits who also occupy similar bodies.

OF TISSUES AND ISSUES

A man complains bitterly, "There's no justice in this world!" What is he talking about? If it doesn't exist on earth, he has obviously never had any contact with the quality of justice that he is complaining ought to be here but isn't. How does he know it is missing in human experience? Why is he sure it exists? Where could that be, and how does he know about it? How does he even have the concept of "justice" (or of grace, truth, holiness, or selfless love) if he is only the material of his body and has had no physical contact with justice by sight, hearing, taste, touch, or smell? Indeed, justice has none of these physical qualities. It is unquestionably nonphysical. That we understand nonphysical concepts proves that we, our real selves that exist independent of our bodies, must be nonphysical as well.

Materialism simply won't hold up to examination. It cannot explain even the simplest realities of life that we experience daily. Much less can materialism explain profound thoughts, philosophical concepts, the drive to expand one's knowledge, and the yearning for purpose and meaning even beyond this physical life. Undeniably, the appreciation of truth, wisdom, and beauty, the loathing of evil, and the longing for ultimate fulfillment do not arise from any quality of the atoms, molecules, or cells that constitute the body or even of the brain.

Tissues know nothing about issues. There is therefore good reason to believe that the spirit to which these undeniably *spiritual* capacities belong will continue to exist even when the tissues that make up the body it has inhabited have died.

The Evidence for Conscience

There is no denying the fact that, even though we have never seen it on earth, each of us innately recognizes a perfect standard of absolute justice, truth, and moral purity. Moreover, we have something we call a "conscience" that tells us when we have violated that standard. We can learn to turn a deaf ear to this inner voice or to pervert it, but it is there nevertheless. Once again, the conscience can only be explained on the basis that there is, residing in these physical bodies, a non-material spirit made in the image of a personal Creator who is a Spirit and has impressed His standards upon us. And it can only be from Him that the obviously spiritual capabilities we possess originate.

The God who inspired the Bible claims to have written His moral laws in every human conscience:

> *For when the Gentiles, which have not the law, do by nature the things contained in the law, these, having not the law, are a law unto themselves: Which show the work of the law written in their hearts, their conscience also bearing witness, and their thoughts the mean while accusing or else excusing one another. (Romans 2:14-15)*

The consciousness of having broken an unseen but not unknown *perfect* standard of right and wrong goes beyond culture and cannot be explained in terms of learned behavior. We can *reason* about what is right and wrong and decide upon behavior totally at odds with our upbringing and presumed conditioning. This fact is proved again and again as generation after generation rebels against the standards they have been taught. The hippies of the sixties are but one example.

Sin is defined in the Bible as coming short of that perfection for which God created us in order to reflect His own glory. As C. S. Lewis put it, "We are mirrors whose only brightness, if we are bright at all, depends entirely upon the sun that shines upon us." Sin is rejecting God's light, refusing to let it guide and energize us in obeying our Creator's will. We know when we are guilty of that, and that disturbing sense of coming short is what troubles the conscience.

Conscience? Yes, we all have an undeniable inner recognition of right or wrong. The man who complains about the injustice of a court decision need not be referring to a violation of any legislated law. In fact, far from accepting every law passed by legislative bodies, we often complain about *their* injustice. The man sitting in court and observing what he considers to be improper procedure and conclusion is really demanding that the court itself adhere to the innate standard that he knows exists and believes the court has violated.

A HIGHER LAW

The courts themselves have always drawn upon that standard. There is no written rule of conduct to cover every situation that might arise. One of the most famous cases decided by the Supreme Court of the United States involved two men and a boy (the only survivors of a ship that sank), drifting for days in a lifeboat. The men decided that it was better to kill the boy than for all three to die for lack of water and sustenance. Evidence produced in court demonstrated that had they not killed the boy, all three indeed would have died. No legislative body had ever written a law to cover such a situation. Nonetheless, the court, drawing upon a higher source of right and wrong, found the two men guilty of murder.

No one has the right to take another's innocent life to save oneself. That rule is written in our conscience. But it is the very opposite of everything that evolution, were it true, would produce as instinctive reaction. Self-preservation is the law of the jungle and enforced by tooth and claw without compassion. Respect for others is highly regarded among humans, and survival of the fittest could never produce it. Everywhere in nature, creatures kill and feed upon one another. We consider that normal and ourselves feed upon lower life forms that we have killed for our sustenance.

"Survival of the fittest" would be undermined by, and could never produce, conscience and ethical concerns.

At the same time, however, we know it is wrong to murder other human beings of whatever color, race, or creed. The random motions of atoms in our brains that presumably all began with a big bang and have proceeded by chance ever since could never produce the moral understanding that is common to all. Nor can moral conviction or compassion for others be explained by any evolutionary process. In fact, "survival of the fittest" would be undermined by, and could never produce, conscience and ethical concerns.

Yet the soldier who falls on an enemy hand grenade to save the lives of his buddies (as some have done), or the policemen and firemen who gave their lives in the attempt to rescue others on September 11, 2001, when the World Trade Center was brought down by terrorists, are admired as heroes. A consistent materialist/evolutionist view would have to denounce as utterly senseless the risking of one's own life to save the lives of total strangers. In spite of the predominant instinct of self-preservation, however, self-sacrificial deeds are admired and given the highest praise by society. How can that be, if we are products of evolution? When did evolution do away with the instinctive law of the jungle that is so essential to survival of the fittest?

REASON VS. CONSCIENCE

Furthermore, in spite of "thou shalt not commit murder" being written indelibly in every conscience, man finds *reasons* to kill and even to torture his fellows. These rationalizations include supposedly justifiable wars, ethnic hatred, and religious fanaticism. Man has his devious explanations by which he can justify almost any evil. He is a *rational* being, even accusing others of being *irrational*, the worst insult one can level at another. But big bangs and the resulting chance motions of atoms do not produce rationality.

Reason is not a quality of matter but an ability of persons. Consequently, a person must consist of something more than the material of the body. Nor can a physical universe explain the existence of personal beings with the ability to reason about their origin. That could come about only through an infinite Being having created them in His image and likeness so that they could know and love Him and one another and receive His and others' love. That we recognize a love that puts others ahead of oneself as the highest experience—and that the expression of human love involves not just the physical pleasure of an animal body, but something so far beyond it that it can only be described as spiritual—is further proof of man's origin at the hand of God and that man is more than the physical composition of his body.

That the expression of human love involves not just the physical pleasure of an animal body, but something so far beyond it that it can only be described as spiritual—is further proof of man's origin at the hand of God.

The very fact that we have a conscience apart from culture and an innate sense of justice that does not derive from man's laws but even complains about their injustices, can only be explained in one way: our spirits living in these bodies were created in the spiritual image of the God who is perfect in justice, holiness, love, truth, and those other nonphysical attributes that only God could possess in flawless fullness. This innate realization is like an echo from a distant and lost paradise of perfection that we know must exist though we've never experienced it. And whenever these moments of insight are honestly faced, we feel a haunting emptiness that seems to be saying that we were created for an excellence somehow lost to our race.

Lenin's Dilemma

Even Lenin could not escape this realization. Boasting that communism was "scientific atheistic materialism," Lenin foolishly insisted that man was a physical stimulus-response organism and that all he could know was through the stimulus of physical phenomena. Lenin was correct, however, in this: that we cannot even think of anything that doesn't exist. This is easily proved by the fact that we cannot imagine a new prime color for the rainbow. We can think of "pink elephants," but pink and elephants both exist. Even the extraterrestrial creatures portrayed on the screen in the most fantastic science fiction and space odyssey movies are merely corruptions or bizarre combinations of creatures and humans we know from earth experience.

Then how do we have the concept of God? If the only thought or understanding we can hold must be aroused by the stimulus of some physical object, what physical stimulus evokes the idea of God, whom we understand to be the ultimate nonphysical Being? Obviously, there is no such physical stimulus. We could not possibly invent God. Then what was it that aroused the idea of God in the human mind, an idea beyond anything physical we have ever observed?

The very fact that we have concepts of spirit beings...is proof that some reality beyond the physical dimension has been able to establish itself in human consciousness.

Lenin couldn't answer that question without abandoning his atheism and materialism, which he refused to do in spite of abundant evidence to the contrary. The same holds true for Satan, angels, demons, and discarnate human spirits. The very fact that we have concepts of spirit beings—and that this awareness has no origin in the material universe—is proof that some reality beyond the physical dimension has been able to establish itself in human consciousness. The evidence is overwhelming that the death of the body is not the end of human existence nor of human experience; it is the release of the human soul and spirit from the earthly connection to its physical body into a purely spiritual dimension.

A STRANGE ANOMALY

Inasmuch as our existence continues after the death of the body, we dare not approach death without absolute certainty as to what lies beyond. Nor is there any time to waste. We don't have the option of deciding when we are ready to die. Death comes calling upon us when it will, and that could happen at any moment. Logically, the very fact that we are spirit beings who—although living in temporary physical bodies—may well exist *eternally* demands great urgency in determining our future with complete certainty.

How astonishing, then, that so few take death seriously enough to investigate thoroughly what lies beyond, and instead seem content to rely upon little more than their own casual opinion. Nor is it any less amazing that so many of those who do concern themselves with the question of what lies beyond death's door are willing to trust their eternal destiny to the word of a Joseph Smith, Mary Baker Eddy, eastern guru, priest, pope, pastor, psychological counselor, seminary, or university professor. Only a fool would step out into eternity trusting his own or another's invented hopes.

Only a fool would step out into eternity trusting his own or another's invented hopes.

2

Of God *and* Human Destiny

Before the mountains were brought forth,
or ever thou hadst formed the earth
and the world, even from everlasting
to everlasting, thou art God.

—Psalm 90:2

Eternity. What does it mean, and why should one even embrace the concept, particularly with regard to human destiny? We know from personal experience and simple observation that material things wear out. The second law of thermodynamics tells us that the entire universe is wearing out, running down like a wind-up toy, and will not last indefinitely. Obviously then, it must have had a beginning, exactly as the Bible declares.

We know that the sun has not been in the sky forever or it would have burned out by now. The same is true of every other sun. Very clearly, there was a time when this universe did not exist; nothing existed, not even the energy out of which the universe seems to be made.

THE INADEQUACY OF A FORCE

Why couldn't the universe have its source in some mysterious cosmic energy that existed from eternity past? The answer is simple—because of the second law of thermodynamics, the law of entropy. Energy could not have existed forever, building up to a "big bang" that created the stars and planets. It would have entropied before it "banged"—and explosions do not create order. Had the universe been here forever, everything should now be the same temperature; heat always moves to something cooler.

Furthermore, energy has neither the intellect nor personal qualities to bring about the incredible design in life and the existence of personal beings. Intelligence and personality are nonphysical and could not have arisen out of energy or matter, so must have preceded them.

Not some force, but a personal being of infinite intelligence and without beginning must have designed and created the universe. This is not the impersonal "first cause" of philosophy, or the competing, capricious, and evolving "gods" of paganism, much less the "Force" of Star Wars. The Creator can only be the "I AM" who revealed Himself to Moses at the burning bush (Exodus

3:14), the self-existent One without beginning or end, of whom Moses in the Bible says, "From everlasting to everlasting, thou art God" (Psalm 90:2).

Obviously, intellect and personality are entirely different from matter and not the stuff out of which it is made. Therefore, the universe is neither part of God nor an extension of God. This means that everything we can see, whether with the naked eye, with a telescope, or with an electron microscope, came from nothing. That is impossible, but we are driven to this conclusion by logic itself. To imagine, however, that life and intelligence sprang spontaneously of its own initiative and power from dead, empty space would be totally irrational. Therefore, something other than the universe and its components must have always existed.

Intelligence and personality are non-physical and could not have arisen out of energy or matter...

THE NECESSITY OF AN INFINITE PERSON

No, not *something* but *Someone,* without beginning or end. But why *Someone?* It is self-evident that the universe, from the structure of the atom, space, and galaxies, to a cell, the smallest living unit, exhibits order and a magnificent intricacy of design that only an infinite intelligence could have planned and put together. It is axiomatic that no thing or force or "higher power" has the ability to think and plan and organize. Furthermore, the human race is composed of individual personalities who possess the ability to conceive conceptual ideas, express them in words or designs, and turn them into intricate structures foreign to nature. They have the ability, as well, to experience love and hate, joy and sorrow, justice and injustice, and to reason about their very existence and destiny.

Only an infinite Person could create persons. So once again we are driven by evidence and logic to conclude that this universe could have come into existence only at the command of Someone who had no beginning, Someone who always existed, and who innately possesses the infinite genius and power to bring everything and everyone into existence *out of nothing*. Certainly not from the superstition current in Egypt in his day, but by divine Revelation, Moses declared: "Before...ever thou hadst formed the earth...even from everlasting to everlasting, thou art God.... A thousand years in thy sight are but as yesterday when it is past, and as a watch in the night" (Psalm 90:2,4).

Rather than an irrational leap, [faith] is a rational step that follows the evidence and logic as far as reason is able...

This is not the god of paganism, of indigenous religions, or of any of the major world religions such as Buddhism (very few Buddhists believe in God), Hinduism, Islam, and others, but the God of the Bible, who uniquely qualifies to be the Creator of all. For reasons that will become clear, we do not consider Christianity to be one of the world's religions but distinct from and contradictory to all of them.

The Bible never tries to prove God's existence. It simply states it as a fact. Nor does the Bible attempt to explain what is beyond our ability to comprehend. It simply declares in its very first verse, "In the beginning God created the heaven and the earth" (Genesis 1:1). In gratitude to the God who had made him, David said, "I will praise thee; for I am fearfully and wonderfully *made*: marvelous are thy *works*; and that my soul knoweth right well" (Psalm 139:14).

Science has not been able, nor will it ever be able, either to verify, to refute, or to improve upon that declaration. We cannot understand it but are asked to accept it by faith. And here we have an example of what faith is: rather than an irrational leap, it is a rational step that follows the evidence and logic as far as reason is able, then takes another step beyond reason—but always and only in the direction that evidence and reason have pointed.

The Bible puts it like this: "Through faith we understand that the worlds were framed by the word of God, so that things which are seen were not made of things which do appear" (Hebrews 11:3). Some have called this the first statement of the atomic theory. No, it is not theory; it is a statement of fact from God himself. Be careful, however, not to read more into this verse than it actually says. It does not say that everything is made out of something invisible. It doesn't, in fact, say that the universe is made out of anything.

THE COMING "BIG BANG"

What Hebrews 11:3 tells us is that the visible universe was not made out of anything visible, for that would mean that something visible always existed and the universe was simply manufactured from materials at hand. On the contrary, that could not be the way it came about, because nothing visible is eternal. Any "material," therefore, would have entropied during the endless time before it was allegedly used to create the universe—and who might have done that? In fact, the universe was created by the Word of God: "God said, Let there be..." (Genesis 1:3,6,9, and so on), and everything that is visible came into existence in obedience to His Word. That same Word, which created all and holds all together, will speak again, and all that is visible in the old creation will dissolve back into nothing:

> *But the heavens and the earth, which are now, by the same word [by which they were created] are kept in store, reserved unto fire against the day of judgment and perdition of ungodly men. (2 Peter 3:7)*

The English translation, "kept in store" and "in Him all things consist" (Colossians 1:17) have the connotation in the Greek of being "held together." Peter goes on to describe the destruction of the universe as being "dissolved" in a "fervent heat" that will burn up the very elements. The English word, "dissolved," is translated from the Greek *luo*, which in its forty-six usages in the New Testament denotes a loosing, or letting go, of something being held together—a scientifically accurate description of the loosing of the force binding the nucleus of the atom together.

All matter is made of atoms, which consist of negatively charged electrons orbiting around a nucleus composed of positively charged protons and neutrally charged neutrons. The electrons are of course held in orbit by the positively charged nucleus—but what holds the nucleus together, since its protons ought to repel one another?

Physicists hypothesize a mysterious "strong force," or "cosmic glue," which overcomes the electromagnetic repulsion that otherwise would push the protons apart and destroy the atom. Without this mysterious force, the very elements of the entire universe would dissolve in one giant ball of fire—exactly as Peter describes.

Long before the second law of thermodynamics had been discovered, Jesus put it very clearly: "Heaven and earth shall pass away" (Matthew 24:35). The universe, however, is not destined to simply wear out due to the passage of untold billions of years. Under the inspiration of the Holy Spirit, Peter explained that all life on earth as we have known it will be summarily terminated, and the entire universe will be destroyed by God in judgment of man's and Satan's rebellion. In its place, a new universe will be created:

> *On the day of judgment...the heavens shall pass away with a great noise, and the elements shall melt with fervent heat, the earth also and the works that are therein shall be burned up.... The heavens being on fire shall be dissolved.... Nevertheless we, according to his promise, look for new heavens and a new earth, wherein dwelleth righteousness. (2 Peter 3:7-13)*

The word "heavens" is used in two ways in Scripture: for all that is physical in dimensional space beyond earth; and for the nonphysical abode of God, called by Jesus "my Father's house... [of] many mansions" (John 14:2). One is visible and temporal, while the other is invisible and eternal. This visible, temporary universe is not all that exists. There is another dimension of existence that is neither physical nor visible—and it doesn't wear out or grow old with the passage of time, nor can it be destroyed, nor will it ever cease to exist.

3

Of Bodies and Spirits

While we look not at the things which are seen, but at the things which are not seen: for the things which are seen are temporal; but the things which are not seen are eternal.

—2 Corinthians 4:18

Physical bodies inhabit the physical universe—a universe designed specifically for physical life, as indicated by overwhelming scientific evidence (see the appendix for a resource list). That the universe could have evolved by chance is preposterous, as we will shortly see. There is no theory that can explain the origin of energy, the stuff of which all matter is made, so it is absurd to speculate about the origin and presumed evolution of physical bodies when we cannot explain the origin of the matter those bodies comprise.

INTELLIGENCE (THE MIND) IS NOT PHYSICAL

Certainly thoughts and ideas, which are demonstrably not physical, do not originate with matter and therefore could not be explained by any evolutionary theory pertaining to physical bodies. Each nonphysical idea (truth, justice, perfection, right, wrong, etc.)—for which there is no physical description—indisputably has an intelligent source that must likewise be nonphysical. Einstein spoke the obvious when he said that matter cannot organize itself into information.

Nor can intelligence be a mere abstraction. It is not a constant but has personal qualities, and it varies from person to person. Why some people are more intelligent than others is not known, but we do know that intelligence is a quality of personal beings. Therefore, intelligence does not originate with the physical matter in the brain, though the brains of some persons seem to be more suited for certain kinds of thought than those of others. The brain is like a computer that is apparently dependent upon the individual "hardware" inherited from ancestors. But the thoughts themselves, though they energize the brain in order to express themselves in words and actions through the body run by the brain, can only originate from the nonphysical thinker inside. And that thinker is mysteriously connected to its body until separated therefrom by what we call death.

We refer to nonphysical beings as souls or spirits. We would not have thoughts and ideas if we were only physical entities—certainly not thoughts of good and evil, of morals and ethics. The real person inside the body, the person who thinks, decides, chooses, and has a sense of its own separate identity and moral responsibility, must be nonphysical. According to the Bible, man has both a soul and spirit. The former recognizes itself as different from all other beings, and the latter recognizes and can commune with God—or choose not to do so.

The soul and spirit, being nonphysical...obviously inhabit their physical bodies only temporarily.

Physical bodies are, of course, subject to the physical laws governing the universe. Our bodies are subject to the pull of gravity, can be damaged in many ways by impact or disease, and eventually die and deteriorate in the grave, according to the second law of thermodynamics. But the soul and spirit, being nonphysical, are clearly not subject to physical laws. They cannot be part of the physical universe and therefore obviously inhabit their physical bodies only temporarily.

Serious Consequences

Nonphysical beings and the nonphysical dimension to which they belong cannot be detected by physical instruments and are invisible to our physical eyes.

Physical things have temporary existence because of physical laws. We can only conclude that the soul and spirit, being invisible and nonphysical, must be non-temporal, i.e., eternal.

The fact that our bodies are visible and thus temporal, but our souls and spirits are invisible and thus eternal, carries serious consequences. When comparing the short life expectancy on earth to eternity, the only rational choice one can make is to be far more diligent in preparing for the latter than for the former. Therefore, the Bible urges us to give priority to eternity over time. Jesus put it like this:

> *Lay not up for yourselves treasures upon earth, where moth and rust doth corrupt, and where thieves break through and steal: but lay up for yourselves treasures in heaven, where neither moth nor rust doth corrupt, and where thieves do not break through and steal. (Matthew 6:19–20)*

The temporal treasures of earth are composed of visible things; the eternal treasures in heaven, like the soul and spirit that make up our true being, are not visible to our physical eyes. Treasures we lay up on this earth must all be left behind when we leave earth for what lies beyond death's door. The great hope of the Christian is not to amass wealth in this life but to receive an eternal reward in heaven.

Peter described that reward as an "inheritance

incorruptible, and undefiled, and that fadeth not away, reserved in heaven for you, who are kept by the power of God through faith unto salvation ready to be revealed in the last time" (1 Peter 1:4–5). In the resurrection, these bodies that decay in death are exchanged for new "spiritual bodies" (1 Corinthians 15:44), which are both visible and invisible, physical and spiritual, "eternal in the heavens" (2 Corinthians 5:1).

The fact that our bodies are visible and thus temporal, but our souls and spirits are invisible and thus eternal, carries serious consequences.

Paul encouraged Christians to believe, in the midst of persecution and martyrdom, that

> *...our light affliction [suffered in this life on earth], which is but for a moment, worketh for us a far more exceeding and eternal weight of glory; while we look not at the things which are seen, but at the things which are not seen: for the things which are seen are temporal; but the things which are not seen are eternal." (2 Corinthians 4:17–18)*

No one can either refute or improve upon that statement. Everything we can now see is temporary. None of it has existed without beginning, nor will it last forever—but our invisible souls and spirits will. We must therefore make our choices and plans in this life in preparation for the next, recognizing that our visible bodies are only temporary housing for our invisible souls and spirits.

These latter are indestructible and will continue to exist eternally after the body dies and is finally dissolved in the grave. Thus, the most solemn question anyone can face is this: "Where will I spend eternity?"

THE PERFECT SETUP FOR DEMONS

Materialists such as Lenin and Freud and their modern followers attempt to deny all of this. Hardcore materialists, however, are a vanishing breed in the face of mounting evidence uncovered in scientific laboratories around the world for the existence of intelligent beings who have no bodies and yet are interacting with the human race. We document that evidence in detail in two books, *The New Spirituality* and *Occult Invasion,* so we will not duplicate it here.

Indeed, so strong is the evidence for the existence of such entities that many scientists who believe in the false and mathematically impossible theory of evolution (many top scientists recognize it as a fraud) are even suggesting that spirit beings could be the highest form of evolution. This was, for example, the opinion of Robert Jastrow, one of the world's leading astronomers, who identified himself as an agnostic. The founder and for many years director of the Goddard Institute for Space Studies (which played a key role in the Pioneer, Voyager, and Galileo space probes), Jastrow has suggested:

> *Life that is a billion years beyond us may be far beyond the flesh-and-blood form that we would recognize. It may be...disembodied and has escaped its mortal flesh to become something that old-fashioned people would call spirits....Maybe it can materialize and then dematerialize. I'm sure it has magical powers by our standards.*

With all due respect to Jastrow, intelligence is not a quality of matter and therefore could not evolve even if evolution were a scientific fact. Bodies of intelligent beings do not *evolve* into spirits but are each already the home of a soul and spirit. Yet what a perfect setup this theory provides for demons. What more could they ask than to have materialistic scientists attempting to contact extraterrestrial life out in space, which scientists are willing to accept as nonphysical beings that "old-fashioned people would call spirits..."! What would today's scientists call these entities, and how could they be certain of either their identity or of their intentions toward mankind? The methods, machines, and theories of materialistic science cannot evaluate nonphysical entities, no matter what one wants to call them.

Spirit Communication and Drugs

Nor could the existence of the human mind ever be explained by evolution. Far from something physical evolving into a nonphysical entity, intelligent life can *only* be nonphysical, for that is the nature of intelligence. In contrast to the brain (which is a physical organ) the mind, which uses the brain like a computer, is nonphysical. Human intelligence can only be explained as a creation of God in His moral and spiritual image and thus with similar capabilities of thought and choice and love, but on a finite human level. We are not physically in God's image, because God, as Jesus said, "is a Spirit" (John 4:24). Rather, we are spirit, soul, and mind in His image.

The fact that nonphysical and nonhuman intelligences exist and are communicating with mankind has been the conviction and experience of primitive peoples since the beginning of time—and now science agrees.

The fact that nonphysical and nonhuman intelligences exist and are communicating with mankind has been the conviction and experience of primitive peoples since the beginning of time—and now science agrees. Through the use of the "sacred mushroom" or peyote or other psychoactive plants, indigenous peoples have always made contact with spirit beings as part of their religious rituals. The use of psychedelic drugs within the last fifty years sparked a revival of paganism in the Western world. Through drugs, multitudes of Westerners were initiated into another dimension inhabited by spirit entities and to the occult and Eastern philosophy that these beings consistently teach.

The phenomenon known as "channeling," whereby nonmaterial intelligences speak through human instruments, has been verified to be genuine (though there are phonies involved as well). One verification is in the fact that the messages that come independently through thousands of different channelers around the world (there are more than 1,000 in Los Angeles alone), in spite of no contact and no exchange of notes with one another, have an undeniable agreement that can only be explained as coming from a common nonhuman source.

The Sorcerer's New Apprentices

Terrence McKenna, who succeeded Timothy Leary as the foremost champion of drugs for the purpose of supposedly "raising consciousness," has traveled the world sampling psychoactive plants of all kinds and documenting their effects. He discovered that all of these substances were able to open contact with nonphysical entities who, says McKenna, "are trying to teach us something." Indeed, that appears to be their insidious purpose.

Moreover, the philosophy they communicate conforms precisely to the four lies with which the Bible says the serpent (Satan) deceived Eve in the Garden of Eden: 1) God is not personal but a Force; 2) There is no death; we don't die but survive in the spirit world (or get recycled in reincarnation); 3) We are evolving into gods; and 4) That process can be accelerated through initiation into secret knowledge with a dark and light side. There is no explaining away as mere coincidence this common message or its conformity to what the serpent taught Eve. On the contrary, it provides absolute proof of both the reality of such spirit communications and their true identity as demonic messengers of Satan indoctrinating mankind with what the Bible calls "doctrines of devils."

The New Testament comes down severely against something it calls "sorcery." The Greek word translated as "sorcery" in English is *pharmakeia*—from which, of course, we get our word for pharmacy, or drugs. We are told in the Bible that this practice of contacting the spirit world through drugs will permeate civilization in the last days. The world will refuse to repent of it and, as a result God's judgment, will fall: "Neither repented they of...their sorceries...for by thy sorceries were all nations deceived...for without [excluded from heaven] are sorcerers" (Revelation 9:21; 18:23; 22:15). Paul warned:

> *Now the Spirit [of God] speaketh expressly, that in the latter times some shall depart from the faith, giving heed to seducing spirits, and doctrines of devils; speaking lies in hypocrisy; having their conscience seared with a hot iron. (1 Timothy 4:1–2)*

Among the "doctrines of devils" taught by these seducing spirits are the other two theories propounded to escape God's judgment after death. We mentioned them briefly in the first chapter. Let us consider first of all what is commonly called "spirit survival." Some of these communicating entities claim to be the spirits of persons who once lived on earth and died centuries or even thousands of years ago. They offer as "proof" bits of information known only to the dead person and the living relative or friend to whom the "spirit" now speaks through a medium. Of course, that does not provide foolproof identification of the "spirit" as being that of the deceased. On the contrary, we know these are "demons" impersonating deceased persons because they promote Satan's basic lies given to Eve in the Garden. Specifically, spirit survival comes from Satan's assertion, "Ye shall not surely die" (Genesis 3:4).

The Bible repeatedly forbids any attempt to communicate with the dead...Necromancy is...trafficking with demons.

No wonder, then, that the Bible repeatedly forbids any attempt to communicate with the dead (Leviticus 20:6; Deuteronomy 18:9-12). Their spirits are either in heaven or hell, not flitting about on the so-called astral plane, communicating with those still alive on earth. Necromancy is, in fact, trafficking with demons, the very "seducing spirits" of which the Holy Spirit warns us throughout Scripture.

SPIRITISM'S ATTRACTIVE APPEAL

Nevertheless, some of the information passed on is extremely convincing, and the lies are irresistibly appealing. Who wouldn't want to believe that there is neither death nor judgment and that we all have within us at our disposal infinite god-like powers if we only knew how to tap into them—a fantasy that these entities promote? Consequently, spiritism has had a great many followers since the beginning of time. Even today, this satanic delusion has hundreds of millions of adherents worldwide. It has always been the prevailing religious belief among indigenous peoples everywhere on earth.

Spirit survival must be rejected because it contradicts our innate concept of perfect justice and because there is absolutely no verifiable evidence to support it.

Claiming to have survived death and to be speaking from "the other side," these seducing spirits allege that after leaving their dead physical bodies, they faced no judgment but were accepted unconditionally by some higher being or white light—regardless of what they had done in their lives on earth. They further allege that after death one continues to live in a spirit world, where one learns further lessons and progresses ever higher. From such communications, the belief in "spirit survival" has arisen. Not only indigenous peoples but many top leaders of the greatest nations in history (and in our modern world as well), such as Queen Victoria and Abraham Lincoln, have been devout believers.

A major problem with this theory is that it includes no accountability or punishment for past deeds. A Hitler presumably fares no worse than a Mother Teresa, except that it will take him longer to realize his alleged true potential. This version of "life after death," in effect, offers an escape through death from the very justice that our courts otherwise would have meted out on earth and that mankind's sense of right and wrong knows should be imposed by the ultimate Judge. That spiritism allows and condones this escape is an offense to the innate sense of justice we all possess.

Moreover, there is no evidence that anyone will "progress" in the spirit world. Why should one's behavior improve there from what it was here, especially in the absence of the motivation that might be supplied if there were serious consequences for evil? Spirit survival must be rejected because it contradicts our innate concept of perfect justice and because there is absolutely no verifiable evidence to support it.

WHAT ABOUT REINCARNATION?

Closely related to spirit survival is a belief in reincarnation, also called transmigration of souls, another one of the "doctrines of devils" that the "seducing spirits" persuasively teach. Devotees reject the biblical teaching that "it is appointed unto men once to die, but after this the judgment" (Hebrews 9:27). Instead, there are allegedly many deaths and rebirths, because after death one's spirit enters the body of a newborn baby to live another life and die again—and another after that, and yet another, and so on, until one has progressed enough to escape the need to return again to earth's physical plane.

The Dalai Lama, for example, claims to be the fourteenth reincarnation of the original Dalai Lama of Tibet. Is there any proof? Only that he was born in Tibet very close to the time of death of the alleged thirteenth Dalai Lama. Nevertheless, this outrageous claim is accepted worldwide, and he is hailed as a leading ambassador for world peace and religious unity. And how does he propose to bring peace to the world? Wherever he travels, the Dalai Lama initiates multitudes into Tibetan Tantric Deity Yoga, promising thereby (as the serpent promised Eve) to make initiates into gods who can create their own universe. For that grandiose promise (which he has never been able to realize, nor have those to whom he makes it) he was given the Nobel Peace Prize! The world takes him so seriously that wherever he goes he is celebrated and received by dignitaries and heads of state. Yet the Dalai Lama (like Hindu gurus and all the other self-proclaimed gods) needs an umbrella to keep off the rain, gets hungry and eats, tires and sleeps, is subject to disease and weakness due to advancing age, and will eventually die. He has never been able to come even close to duplicating the miracles of Christ or offer any evidence that

Karma...punishes evil with the same evil, and thereby perpetuates it. Reincarnation is thus amoral and can be dismissed on that basis alone...

his claims to deity are valid—or to enable those he initiates into deity to manifest any god-like qualities.

In contrast to spirit survival, reincarnation includes the concept of punishment in the next life, imposed by something called "the law of Karma." The judgment it imposes, however, is without mercy and offers neither solution nor hope. In fact, Karma produces more evil in the process of supposedly punishing it. Indeed, it punishes evil with the same evil, and thereby perpetuates it. Reincarnation is thus amoral and can be dismissed on that basis alone, as well as its being senseless and hopeless.

The Amorality of Reincarnation

Let us consider its amorality first. The horrible truth is that, rather than offering a solution to evil, reincarnation perpetuates evil. Both Karma and reincarnation work according to the alleged "law of cause and effect." Yes, the Bible, too, says, "whatsoever a man soweth, that shall he also reap" (Galatians 6:7). But that phrase is preceded by the words "God is not mocked," indicating that it is man's Creator—not an impersonal force—who causes him to reap what he sows.

Furthermore, according to the Bible, the "reaping" of the consequences of past deeds is not fatalistic as it is in reincarnation, but God offers an escape by way of His grace and forgiveness. The God of the Bible loves the sinner and has provided pardon from punishment, and He has done so on a righteous and judicially just basis.

Instead of leaving man to suffer under an impersonal law of Karma, God loves us so much that He came as a man through the virgin birth to where we were, in order to share in the trials of this life and to pay the penalty demanded by His own infinite justice for our rebellion. The Bible, therefore, is able to offer redemption and forgiveness of all sins to all who will receive God's gracious pardon on His terms—something reincarnation does not and cannot do.

In contrast, according to the law of Karma, a man who beats his wife in this life must return in the next life as a wife beaten by her husband. But the husband who beats the former wife beater, who is now a wife, must himself come back in yet another life as a wife beaten by her husband, and so on. There is no escape from this karmic sentence. Thus, a thief or murderer must become the victim of the same crime. That the perpetrator of each crime must become the victim of the same crime means there must be another perpetrator, who must become the victim of yet another perpetrator, *ad infinitum, ad absurdum.* Instead of solving the problem of evil, reincarnation perpetuates it and is therefore amoral.

Senseless and Hopeless

Reincarnation is also senseless. Who remembers the details of mistakes made and costly lessons presumably learned in prior lives? No one. Then what is the point of coming back to live on earth again and again if one has no way of knowing whether lessons have been learned and progress is being made? Moreover, the increasing evil on earth proves that progress is not being made. The very concept of reincarnation is therefore senseless.

It is also hopeless. Supposedly the "bad karma" (whatever that means) that we build up in this life requires another life to "work it off." But in that very process we build up more bad karma, which requires yet another life, then another life, and so on endlessly. This is why the Hindu refers to "the wheel of reincarnation" (it just keeps rolling on endlessly), and Gandhi called it "a burden too great to bear."

The increasing evil on earth proves that progress is not being made...the very concept of reincarnation is therefore senseless.

What is happening to us in this life is presumably due to the karma of a prior life; but that was due to the karma of yet a prior life and so forth forever into the past. Going back through endless numbers of prior lives, one finally reaches the point when the three *gunas* of "God" were in perfect balance in the void. Inexplicably, something unknown caused an imbalance. As a result, the *prakriti* (manifestation) began, and here we are, reaping the results of bad karma that began in "God," is locked into the very fabric of the universe, and can never be escaped! Reincarnation, therefore, is hopeless.

There is not a shred of evidence to support reincarnation. It is rather a lie of the Serpent to prevent mankind from facing the reality of God's righteous judgment and accepting the forgiveness He offers. The few examples of people here and there who seem to have a fragmentary memory from a prior existence break down upon closer examination. Even those alleged memories are insufficient to form the basis for progress in their own lives, let alone for the entire human race. Being amoral, senseless, and hopeless, and lacking any substantive evidence to support it, reincarnation must be rejected.

We are eternal beings who will spend eternity somewhere. Where will it be? And how can we know?

We are eternal beings who will spend eternity somewhere. Where will it be? And how can we know? There is no more important question to be faced and answered.

4

IN SEARCH *of the* TRUE FAITH

But to him that worketh not, but believeth on him that justifieth the ungodly, his faith is counted for righteousness.

—ROMANS 4:5

IT IS ASTONISHING how many millions of otherwise seemingly intelligent people are willing to risk their eternal destiny upon less evidence than they would require for buying a used car. Thomas Hobbes, for example, a seventeenth-century philosopher and mathematician, who spent years analyzing the evil in man and attempting to find a social system to bring universal peace in this brief life, failed to make adequate investigation and preparation for the next life that will never end. Consequently, as death approached, he made this sad confession, "Now I am about to take my last voyage, a great leap in the dark." It seems irrational to take a leap into the dark in any direction—but into *eternity*?

Omar Khayyam viewed death as the door of darkness to "the road which to discover we must travel too." But it's too late once one has passed through that "door" onto that unknown road. Thus, Shakespeare suggested that "in that sleep of death what dreams may come when we have shuffled off this mortal coil, must give us pause." But more than "pause" to reflect, we need certainty and we need it now, backed not by wishful thinking but by solid evidence.

RELIGIOUS "FAITH"

Whatever expectations people entertain of life after death, such beliefs are generally categorized as part of their religion. Another word for religion is "faith," and by that definition, there are many "faiths" in the world. "People of faith" (a term used for those who hold to some religious belief) are joining together in political and social action, supposedly to make a better world. President Bush originated what he calls the "Faith-Based and Community Initiatives," which recognize all "faiths" as apparently equally valid.

This cooperation to improve society for mutual benefit has brought a new tolerance for all religions, no matter how contradictory their opposing views. And here we face another anomaly: according to recent polls, a surprisingly high percentage (the majority among both Catholics and Protestants) of those who identify themselves with a particular religion nevertheless believe that many other religions, if not all, will also take their followers to whatever "heaven" they offer.

Religion is called faith because it is something most people imagine they are expected to believe, regardless of proof. Ask most religious people why they believe what they believe, and they would be at a loss to explain. More than likely, their response would be to say loyally (for some, stubbornly) something like, "I was born a Baptist, and I'll die a Baptist"; or, "I was born a Catholic and I'll die a Catholic," or Methodist, Hindu, Buddhist, Muslim, atheist. Yet very few can give a valid reason why they believe what they believe (or don't believe), and many are offended when asked for one.

Ask most religious people why they believe what they believe, and they would be at a loss to explain.

Right here we find something very odd. As noted above, most people are less careful when it comes to eternity than they are about buying a car or checking the labels for exact ingredients of foodstuffs, or for almost anything else in this life. This is evident from the weak reasons that are usually offered by those who attempt to justify their religious faith: "I like the pastor"; or, "The choir is fantastic"; or, "The people are so friendly"; or, "It's the closest church"; or, "They have a wonderful youth program"; or, "Our family has always belonged to this denomination"; or, "Some missionaries came to the door and invited us to attend and we weren't going anywhere, so...." In view of the fact that one's eternal destiny is at stake, it is incomprehensible that so few people really get serious about faith.

A Call to Re-examine Your Faith

Unquestionably, there is nothing more important than having an impeccably factual and rational basis for one's faith. To the many who think of faith as a belief strongly held and without evidence to support it (and often even in spite of much evidence to the contrary), that may seem an outrageous statement. Logically, however, if believing something strongly doesn't make it so (as human experience daily proves), then it is the greatest folly to continue on with a "faith" that has no basis in fact but merely in fancy—and must therefore inevitably prove to be empty. The cost could be eternal and irrecoverable.

That being the case, how much better it is to "lose" one's faith now while there is still time to discover the truth, than to find out too late that one has been following a lie. Such disillusionment often follows when a young person matures, leaves home to work or attend university or enter the armed services, and is no longer under parental and church influence. This could be the case whether one were a Buddhist, Hindu, Muslim, or an adherent of any other religion.

The same holds true for someone who has claimed to be a Christian but has no personal relationship with Christ on His terms. That there are millions of such people is evident from the answers given on various religious polls.

Many a young person raised in a Christian home, having professed faith in Christ, and having long attended and even been active in a good evangelical church, has later rejected Christ on the basis of peer pressure, or a little "higher education," or out of necessity to justify a godless lifestyle. This turning away from one's professed faith is often justified with the claim that there is no truth, but that we have all, no matter what the religion, simply been conditioned to believe what we believe.

The idea of conditioning is a myth that must be dispensed with in our search for true faith.

Since the days of Freud, psychology has long promoted the theory that any religious faith is merely a conditioned response learned especially in youth. That may well be true in many cases, but it cannot serve as justification for abandoning what one has been taught from childhood. The issue is whether what one was persuaded to believe is the *truth* or not. Tragically, the truth has often been abandoned for a more appealing lie.

In fact, this idea of conditioning is a myth that must

be dispensed with in our search for true faith. The very fact that the person has rebelled against his upbringing and alleged conditioning is itself proof that this theory is false. That multitudes of formerly religious persons offer what they consider to be *sound reasons* for rejecting what they have been taught and once believed proves that the so-called conditioning upon which this theory rests didn't work, at least not in their cases. The very rebellion the theory has been adopted to excuse *disproves* the conditioning theory.

DARWINISM'S INNATE MEANINGLESSNESS

Darwin faced a similar problem, which still haunts evolutionists to this day. If we are simply the product of chance motions of atoms, beginning with an inexplicable explosion (of an unknown energy source) called "the big bang," then all of our thoughts are simply the result of chance motions of atoms in our brains and are thus without meaning—and that includes the theory of evolution itself. Evolution denies that the very theory of evolution can have any meaning and therefore be true. Evolutionists insist that whatever is going on in our brain cells at any moment must be traced back to that huge explosion, following which lifeless matter somehow came to life and, over eons of time, eventually evolved into human brain cells. There is no point in this process at which meaning could have been introduced, nor is there any rational source within matter or energy (they are interchangeable) from which a purposeful plan could have come.

Science can tell neither *where* the energy came from that was involved in the alleged big bang, nor *why* the explosion occurred, nor *how* it could have produced order. Indeed, if all we have to deal with is exploding energy, then to ask why or how (which imply meaning) is useless. There is no *why* or *wherefore* in energy and explosions. Shut down all universities and seminaries, and sit in mourning: there is no truth, no purpose, no meaning, no basis for morals or ethics, no right or wrong. Nor would we mourn at all for missing truth and meaning if we were merely the product of an explosion of energy, for neither such concepts nor the sense that they were missing would ever result from random motions of atoms in our brains.

There is no point in the [evolutionary] process at which meaning could have been introduced, nor is there any rational source within matter or energy from which a purposeful plan could have come.

It is undeniable that there is neither truth, meaning, nor purpose without an intelligent Creator who, for His own reasons, made the universe and each of us in His image. Yet the world of academia largely rejects this inescapable fact, because it does not want to be accountable to God. Professors and students claim to be on a quest for truth while denying that it exists or that anyone could identify it if it did. Such is the nihilistic atmosphere in major universities around the world. It is considered to be too dogmatic for anyone to claim that truth can be known. Then what is the point of research and study, if all we can achieve is a listing of differing opinions, none of which can be declared to be either right or wrong?

The Destructive Liberalism of Much Theology

This attitude has even found its way into theological seminaries and has spilled over from there into the thinking of most religious people. It is now considered presumptive or triumphalistic to suggest that there is only one true faith and that all others are wrong. That would be inexcusably offensive to those of other beliefs. As a result, when seeking to impress upon the average person the necessity of knowing for certain that one is following the right spiritual path into eternity, one hears repeatedly the popular response delivered with a shrug of the shoulders, "Aren't we all taking different roads to get to the same place?"

Although that sounds sufficiently broad-minded to avoid offending anyone, it is actually the ultimate in narrow-mindedness. While it allows everyone to take *different roads,* it insists that they must all end up in the *same place*. According to this dictum, there is only one destination beyond the grave. Once again, in violation of the sense of justice and fairness we all innately possess, a Hitler fares no worse than a Mother Teresa. And those who suggest the contrary quickly find that this broadminded tolerance is intolerant of any opinion that disagrees with it.

In an ancient form of this modern delusion, the Persian scriptures declare, "Whatever road I take joins the highway that leads to Thee....Broad is the carpet God has spread." Jesus, too, spoke of a broad road that sounds very much like this "all roads" and "broad carpet" concept. However, far from commending it, He said it leads to destruction: "Broad is the way, that leadeth to destruction, and many there be which go in thereat: because strait is the gate, and narrow is the way, which leadeth unto life, and few there be that find it" (Matthew 7:13–14).

Jesus was not so dogmatic and narrow-minded as to say there is only one destination for all; He said there are two—heaven and hell. No one will be forced to go to either. Which of the two roads one takes is a matter of individual choice. Of course, if we choose to take the narrow road to God, it must be on His terms.

The Unpopularity of Conviction

In an interesting essay in *Time* magazine (June 15, 1998), its author related an experience that illustrates the foolishness of today's unwillingness to take a definite stand when it comes to religious belief:

> *As I checked in for a test at a local hospital the admissions lady inquired, "What is your religious preference?" I was tempted to repeat what Jonah said, "I am a Hebrew, ma'am. And I fear the Lord, the God of Heaven…." But that would have got me sent to psychiatry rather than x-ray….*
>
> *In ancient times, they asked, "Who is your God?" A generation ago, they asked your religion. Today your creed is a preference. According to Chesterton, tolerance is the virtue of people who do not believe in anything.*
>
> *When it is believed that on your religion hangs the fate of your immortal soul, the Inquisition follows easily; when it is believed that religion is a breezy consumer preference, religious tolerance flourishes. After all, we don't persecute people for their taste in cars. Why for their taste in gods?*
>
> *Oddly, though…there is one form of religious intolerance that does survive…the disdain bordering on contempt for those for whom religion is not a preference but a conviction….*

A conviction that there is a definite way to heaven (and only one) is not tolerated in this day of professed tolerance, because it insists that all roads *don't* lead to the same place, that truth *does* exist, and that there *is* a distinction between what is right and what is wrong. Instead of such antiquated convictions, ecumenical broad-mindedness is the new wave for the new millennium. We are expected to set aside the rational necessity of being certain about our eternal destiny in favor of a mindless tolerance that promises only to avoid religious arguments in this life but offers no sensible assurance for the next.

Tolerance sounds like a virtue, and at times it may be. On the other hand, an attitude allowing a parent to be tolerant of behavior that is harming a child, or the police to be tolerant of criminals who prey upon others, turns virtue into the vice of aiding and abetting evil. Should doctors be tolerant of disease, or public schoolteachers tolerant of any answer on an exam, no matter how wrong? And to be tolerant of a false hope that has deceived multitudes and will lead them to destruction can hardly be the stance of one who truly loves others. This is why Paul said, "Knowing therefore the terror of the Lord, we persuade men (2 Corinthians 5:11).

To be tolerant of a false hope that has deceived multitudes and will lead them to destruction can hardly be the stance of one who truly loves others.

The issue of where one will spend eternity is not a matter of preference, like joining the Elks instead of the Lions. Our opinions and inclinations cannot overturn what God has decreed. Why should the Creator tolerate and admit into His heaven rebels who have broken His laws, trampled on His Word, and rejected the salvation He offers? To imagine that is to credit God with the kind of indulgence of His creatures that we would condemn in a judge in an earthly court of law.

[illegible]RADICTORY BELIEFS CANNOT ALL BE TRUE!

In his landmark book, *The Closing of the American Mind,* Chicago philosophy professor Alan Bloom pointed out that the one virtue in America these days seems to be openness to anything and everything as equally valid behaviors or points of view. Any and every opinion is greeted with equal tolerance—not conviction, but tolerance. It would be unacceptable dogmatism in most circles today to say that truth exists. That would mean that those who did not accept it would be wrong—and no one must be wrong.

Dr. Bloom points out that we have become so open to everything that our minds have been closed to the idea that something may indeed be true and something else false. The closing of the American mind through openness to everything! That is exactly what is happening in the post-rational era that has overtaken our universities and seminaries and the thinking of many church leaders.

Again, simple logic would refute this idea of all roads leading to the same place. If words have any meaning, then we must acknowledge that there are serious contradictions between various world religions. They don't even agree upon the number of gods (millions for Hindus, one for Muslims, none for Buddhists), much less upon their identity or nature. Nor do world religions agree upon how to appease their god or gods—or how to reach their version of heaven after death.

Jesus claimed that He is the only way to heaven: "I am the way, the truth, and the life: no man cometh to the Father, but by me" (John 14:6). He went so far as to say, "All that ever came before me are thieves and robbers," (John 10:8) and that includes Buddha, Confucius, and so on. Christianity stands not only in contrast but in opposition to all of the ways to heaven offered by the world's religions. Christ says they *all* lead to destruction. Surely, because of the grave consequences they convey, His claims deserve careful investigation.

Meeting the Challenge

To make such an investigation was the challenge delivered to Professor Simon Greenleaf, co-founder of the Harvard Graduate School of Law, by some of his students in the mid-1800s. Greenleaf was, according to U.S. Supreme Court Chief Justice Melville W. Fuller, "the highest authority [on legal evidence] cited in our courts." After making an exhaustive examination of the claims of Christ just as he would examine evidence or testimony introduced into a court of law, Greenleaf, who had been a life-long self-professed agnostic, embraced Christ as his Savior and all that the Bible portrays of Him. As a result, he wrote *Testimony of the Evangelists*, in which he declared that the Bible withstood every test of evidence a court of law could impose and challenged fellow members of the legal profession to examine it honestly. Declaring that biblical

Christianity does not seek accommodation with world religions but denounces "all...religion[s] of the world [as]...false...and dangerous," Greenleaf argued:

> *[The claims of] Jesus Christ...solicit the grave attention of all [and] demand their cordial belief as a matter of vital concernment. These are no ordinary claims; and it seems hardly possible for a rational being to regard them with even a subdued interest; much less to treat them with mere indifference and contempt.*
>
> *If not true, they are little else than the pretensions of a bold imposter...but if they are well founded and just they can be no less than the high requirements of heaven, addressed by the voice of God to the reason and understanding of man....*[1]

In contrast to the misinformation deliberately passed on by atheistic professors to university students (and believed by most of the latter), many of the most brilliant scientists in history were as firm believers in the Bible, and in Christ as their personal Savior, as was Greenleaf. If space permitted, we could quote the Christian testimonies of Johann Kepler, the founder of astronomy; Robert Boyle, the father of modern chemistry; John Ray, the father of English natural history, and the greatest zoologist and botanist of his day; Sir Isaac Newton, who invented calculus, discovered the law of gravity and the three laws of motion, anticipated the law of energy conservation, developed the particle theory of light propagation, and invented the reflecting telescope; Carolus Linnaeus, father of biological taxonomy; Michael Faraday, one of the greatest physicists of all time, who developed foundational concepts in electricity and magnetism; Charles Babbage, founder of computer science, who first developed information storage and retrieval systems; John Dalton, the father of atomic theory, which revolutionized chemistry; Gregory Mendel, the father of genetics; Louis Pasteur, the father of bacteriology, who established the germ theory of disease; Lord Kelvin, one of the great physicists of all time, the first to provide a precise statement of the first and second laws of thermodynamics—and a host of other great scientists, ancient and modern.[2]

By lifelong examination of the physical universe, from the innermost depths of the atom to the farthest reaches of space, such men arrived at the same faith in Christ as did Greenleaf. To move to more recent times, Werner Von Braun, the father of space science, wrote:

> *The vast mysteries of the universe should only confirm our belief in the certainty of its Creator. I find it as difficult to understand a scientist who does not acknowledge the presence of a superior rationality behind the existence of the universe as it is to comprehend a theologian who would deny the advances of science.*

Perhaps, however, it would be of interest to see further testimony of fellow members of Greenleaf's own profession from across the Atlantic, who, after careful examination of the evidence, pronounced the testimony of the Bible concerning Christ to be true and received Him as their Lord and Savior. The Chief Justice of England, Lord Darling, once said that "no intelligent jury in the world could fail to bring in a verdict that the resurrection story is true."

Lord Lyndhurst, recognized as one of the greatest legal minds in British history, was in complete agreement with Darling. Solicitor-general of the British government, attorney-general of Great Britain, three times high chancellor of England, and elected as high steward of the University of Cambridge, Lyndhurst held in one lifetime the highest offices ever conferred upon a judge in Great Britain. Concerning the resurrection of Jesus Christ in the light of legal evidence, and why he became a Christian, he wrote: "I know pretty well what evidence is: and I tell you, such evidence as that for the resurrection has never broken down [in any court] yet."

No intelligent jury in the world could fail to bring in a verdict that the resurrection story is true.

Blaise Pascal was one of the greatest philosophers and early mathematicians. He laid the foundations for hydrostatics, hydrodynamics, differential calculus, and the theory of probability. Pascal declared, "I count only two men rational: the man who loves God with all his heart because he has found Him; or the man who seeks

God with all his heart because he has as yet found Him not." He left this challenge for mankind:

> *How can anyone lose who chooses to be a Christian? If, when he dies, there turns out to be no God and his faith was in vain, he has lost nothing—in fact, has been happier in life than his nonbelieving friends. If, however, there is a God and a heaven and hell, then he has gained heaven and his skeptical friends will have lost everything in hell!*

---

1. Simon Greenleaf, *A Treatise on the Law of Evidence* (New York: Arno Press), p. 13.

2. For a larger list and further details, see http://www.innercite.com/~tstout/cs/pog_a.shtml.

5

Shortcut *to* Truth

I have even from the beginning declared
it to thee; before it came to pass
I showed it thee.

—Isaiah 48:5

In spite of the great appeal to many that what one believes can *create* reality, this is clearly a delusion. In fact, belief must be based *upon* reality. Yet the belief of so many, particularly in the area of religion, has no factual foundation. The beliefs of many religious people are little more than sanctified superstitions. Many either do not want to face any evidence to the contrary ("I never discuss religion!") or imagine that faith is proved to be all the stronger if it stands firm in the face of evidence that contradicts it. Obviously, however, a "faith" that is not based upon truth cannot be defended and should not be relied upon. It can only lead one day to taking a final—and eternally fatal—leap into the dark.

Where are truth and certainty to be found? Shall we devote our lives to studying all of the world's religions in an attempt to find the right one? No one could live long enough to complete that task. Then how can one make a valid decision without knowing all of the choices available?

THE UNIQUENESS OF THE BIBLE

There is a simple solution, a shortcut to truth: start with the Bible first and investigate it thoroughly. Why start there? Not just because the Bible claims to be the only inspired Word of the one true God who created us. It also claims that all of the world's religions and their scriptures are false and actually in the service of Satan. The Bible calls Satan "the god of this world" (2 Corinthians 4:4) and thus the author of its religions. So if the Bible is true, we have saved ourselves a lifetime of vain searching through false systems.

In fact, we can prove beyond the shadow of a doubt that every word in the Bible is true. Entire books by many authors offer this proof in detail. We have also presented it extensively in other writings. Here we can only provide enough information for each reader to be able to study further in order to confirm the absolute truth of the Bible to his or her own satisfaction.

The Bible has several unique features not found in the scriptures of the world's religions, making it possible to substantiate its claims. Christianity is not a philosophy, mystical experience, or esoteric practice. Nor are the major doctrines of Christianity a matter of mere dogma and belief. They are intricately tied into established history. In contrast to the world's religions, all of which are based to a large extent upon legends, Christianity alone is based upon undeniable and historical facts. Its doctrines can thus be evaluated on the basis of evidence.

Christianity is not a philosophy, mystical experience, or esoteric practice...In contrast to the world's religions... Christianity alone is based upon undeniable and historical facts.

Furthermore, many of the Bible's major events and teachings were prophesied centuries and even thousands of years beforehand in understandable language. Their actual fulfillment is part of recorded world history. The Bible stands upon a four-fold foundation, every part of which can be examined and verified: 1) prophecy foretelling events and doctrines in advance, 2) fulfillment of those prophecies in detail, 3) secular history testifying to the fulfillment of prophecies and events, and 4) factual data corroborated by archaeology and science. None of this is the case with the teachings or scriptures of any of the world's religions.

Such differences set the Bible apart as absolutely unique. In fact, Christianity, which is based upon the

Bible, cannot even be counted among the religions of the world. Christianity does not seek accommodation, much less ecumenical partnership, with world religions; it seeks their overthrow as hopelessly false and destructive to mankind. That may come as a shock to some readers, but it is the clear teaching of the Bible. Christ himself, as we have already quoted, denounced as "thieves and robbers" all who sought to get to heaven except through Him. Such bold claims cannot be lightly dismissed. They deserve to be carefully evaluated.

COMPARING THE BIBLE'S CLAIMS

Each religion offers a system of belief and practice taught by its founder whereby one supposedly gains acceptance with God. No religion claims that its founder died for the sins of the world and was resurrected. Nor is it essential to any of the world's religions that its founder be alive. Christianity, on the other hand, depends *entirely* upon Christ himself having died for our sins and being resurrected, presently alive, and living by His Spirit within His followers. Jesus said, "Because I live, ye shall live also" (John 14:19).

Another unique feature of the Bible is its authorship. It was written by some forty different men over a period of about 1,600 years. Living in different cultures and at different times in history, most of them never knew one another. Yet the Bible comprises one intricately integrated message from Genesis to Revelation—without any internal contradictions. The continuity and remarkable content of the message can only be explained by inspiration from a supernatural Source. As the Bible grew, subsequent revelations were always consistent with what went before, supplementing, enlarging, and building thereupon.

These forty authors had only this in common: each claimed to be inspired by the one true God. If this claim is not true, the Bible is the greatest fraud imaginable and has done incalculable harm to billions. Yet it bears the unmistakable stamp of truth in many verifiable ways, and its unequaled moral effect for good could hardly be the fruit of fraud.

There is not one word in the Bible that reflects the ignorance or superstition of the culture or the time in which it was written.

The oldest part of the biblical text dates back about 3,500 years and the newest about 1,900 years, yet it remains as valid and relevant as when it was written. Not a word or concept is outdated by the progress of civilization or science. One can find no other literature of the same time period of which that can be said.

There is not one word in the Bible that reflects the ignorance or superstition of the culture or the time in which it was written. Moses, for example, who wrote the first five books of the Bible, lived around 1600 B.C. He was raised in Pharaoh's palace and given the best education available in the Egypt of that day. That means he was schooled in many grossly unscientific notions that were fully believed by Pharaoh's counselors at that time. Yet not one of these errors appears in the writings of Moses. Instead, there is a wisdom and understanding foreign to, and far beyond, the culture of that time—something that could not possibly be the case had he not, as he claimed, been inspired of God in what he wrote.

Scientific Verification

To a large extent, the hygienic laws God gave Israel through Moses preserved Jewish communities during the Middle Ages from the various plagues that swept through the civilized world. Jews were even persecuted because they seemed immune and were therefore accused of putting this curse on the Gentile populace. It took medicine more than 3,000 years to catch up to Moses, even in something so simple as the need to wash one's hands. It was only a few decades ago that the medical profession recognized the preventive health benefits of circumcision, which God gave to Abraham nearly 4,000 years ago. Only recently was it also discovered that on the eighth day after birth, the day prescribed for circumcision, the clotting factor in the newborn's blood, having dropped right after birth, is at the highest level that it will ever be.

The Bible, of course, is not intended to be a science reference manual. It deals with something far more important. It does, however, make many factual statements about the universe that reflect a wisdom far beyond the time and culture in which it was written. Some of these insights have only recently been confirmed by modern science, and none of them has been proved wrong. That in itself is a remarkable witness to inspiration not found in other scriptures.

For comparison, read anything written at the same time that the books of the Old Testament (or of the New) were written. The difference is like night and day. The Qur'an, for example, written more than 2,000 years after the earliest books in the Bible, contains numerous unscientific statements and superstitions, and treats primitive Arab customs in dress and diet of Muhammad's time as inspired by Allah and obligatory upon Muslims even today.

In a day when it was believed that the earth sat on the back of a tortoise floating in a cosmic sea, the Bible said God "hangeth the earth upon nothing" (Job 26:7).

The contrast between other scriptures, which reflect the superstitious, unscientific views of their time, and the supernatural validity of the Bible, cannot be denied. In a day when it was believed that the earth sat on the back of a tortoise floating in a cosmic sea, the Bible said God "hangeth the earth upon nothing" (Job 26:7). What it says about clouds and rain is remarkable: "He [God] bindeth up the waters in his thick clouds...[and maketh] a way for the lightning...to cause it to rain on the earth" (Job 26:8; 38:25–26). Molecules of water are, in fact, *bound* together in a way that is unique among all substances. Indeed, it is this peculiar molecular bonding that allows clouds and raindrops to form. Moreover, as the Bible says, the electric charge connected with lightning plays a key role in causing rain. These facts were only discovered in this century, yet the Bible stated them 3,500 years ago. Many similar examples could be given.

ARCHAEOLOGICAL VERIFICATION

The Bible deals accurately with the history, location, and geography of many nations, countries, and cities. For example, 29 of the ancient kings mentioned in the Bible are also named on monuments of their time, some dating back 4,000 years. Of the 195 consonants in their names, there are only two or three that could be questioned as to whether they are written in the Bible exactly as on the monuments. By comparison, the greatest scholar of his day, the librarian at Alexandria, Egypt, in 200 B.C., refers to 38 Egyptian kings, of which only three or four are recognizable. Of the Assyrian kings he lists, only one is identifiable and it isn't spelled correctly. In the list Ptolemy made of 18 Babylonian kings, not one is spelled properly and none could be identified without help from other sources. Yet in the Bible, each of the 29 kings from 10 countries has his complex name spelled correctly, and each is given his right place and time in history, as verified by ancient monuments discovered by archaeologists.

Such accuracy in every detail reinforces the truth of the doctrines being taught at the same time.

No other scriptures have been critically investigated like the Bible. It has been under the skeptics' microscopes for centuries and analyzed from every conceivable angle by critics determined to discredit it. None of the scriptures of any of the world's religions has been subjected to comparable scrutiny, nor could they withstand it if they were. Even a cursory reading of scriptures other than the Bible reveals multiple errors of fact, history, and science.

Even a cursory reading of scriptures other than the Bible reveals multiple errors of fact, history, and science.

Yes, critics have often claimed to have found errors in the Bible based upon what was known at the time. When further facts have been discovered, however, the Bible has proved to be 100 percent accurate and the critics wrong. For example, earlier in the last century, it was claimed that the Hittite peoples, given prominent mention in the Bible (as strong and numerous from the time of Abraham to David), had never existed. Later, the archaeological evidence began to pour in. Today, there is an entire museum in Ankara, Turkey, devoted to the Hittites and filled with proof that what the Bible said about them was accurate.

Great museums around the world display masses of evidence fully supporting what the Bible has to say. In comparison, consider the Book of Mormon. For decades, at the cost of millions of dollars, the Mormon Church has maintained an aggressive archaeological program literally scouring North, Central, and South America in search of evidence to support the Book of Mormon. To date they have not found so much as a pin or coin or stone or inscription. There is no evidence whatsoever that any of the cities described in the Book of Mormon ever existed. Even the geography can't be verified.

Furthermore, its claim that the American Indians are descended from Jews who came to the uninhabited Americas in about 600 B.C. is disproved by genetics. The video, *DNA vs. The Book of Mormon*, features interviews with geneticists who testify that the DNA of thousands of American Indians, living and dead, from North, Central, and South America, has been examined, and there isn't a drop of Jewish blood in any of them. Their ancestors all came across the Bering Straits from Siberia.

Similar scientific errors, superstitious nonsense, and make-believe "history" are found in the *Bhagavad-Gita* and other Hindu writings, as in the legends of various indigenous peoples around the world. Israeli students, however, study the history of their country and ancestors from the Bible, and archaeologists use the Bible as a guide for locating the buried ruins of ancient cities.

6

Facing the Facts

The fool hath said in his heart, There is no God.

—Psalm 14:1; 53:1

Except ye repent, ye shall all likewise perish.

Luke 13:3,5

Without taking time to explain the many disagreements, it is undeniable that there are such great basic differences between the world's religions that it seems irrational to suggest that they are essentially in agreement and all lead to the same place. Nevertheless, in spite of these differences, there is evidence that those who follow world religions will indeed all end up in the same place—but not where they promise to take their followers. Interestingly, we find in the world's various religious systems the same teachings that are woven throughout the communications (doctrines of devils) to which we have earlier referred as coming from the spirit world.

All religions have in common a universal opposition to the God of the Bible and His gospel concerning salvation by grace and faith alone through Christ Jesus and His sacrifice on the Cross. This commonality places them all on one side—and Christianity on the other.

CHRISTIANITY VS. ALL RELIGIONS

Indeed, so wide is the chasm between Christianity and all the world's religions that it seems equally clear that Christians will definitely arrive at a different eternal destiny from everyone else. Yes, the various religions differ in the details relevant to the appeasement of their particular god or gods and the methods of attaining to *nirvana*, *moksha*, or whatever paradise they may offer. However, they all have in common the belief that their religious goals can somehow be achieved through their own good efforts and/or faithful participation in rituals and sacraments. Whether by yoga or paying off bad karma for the Hindu, or by good deeds for the Muslim (or dying in *jihad* [holy war] or on the *hajj* pilgrimage to Mecca), or through appeasing

All religions have in common a universal opposition to the God of the Bible and His gospel concerning salvation by grace and faith alone through Christ Jesus

the spirits in African tribal religions and Shintoism, or by meditation techniques to escape desire and return to the void for the Buddhist, or by the sacraments of a supposed Christian church—it is all a matter of self-effort, which the God of the Bible firmly tells us He will not accept as even partial payment for having broken His laws.

The Bible clearly states: "But to him that worketh not, but believeth on him that justifieth the ungodly, his faith is counted for righteousness" (Romans 4:5). Jesus said, "I came not to call the righteous, but sinners to repentance" (Mark 2:17). Paul emphasized that point: "Christ Jesus came into the world to save sinners" (1 Timothy 1:15). The world's religions, along with the false Christianity that trusts in works and sacramentalism, attempt to make a person righteous enough for heaven. In contrast, the Bible says that everyone by very nature sins, must confess it, and must believe the gospel to receive forgiveness of sins and thereby be admitted eternally into the true God's presence.

Biblical salvation is by faith, and faith necessarily involves that which is unseen. It is not faith to believe in that which is present in visible form. Faith reaches out to the unseen world of the spirit and the eternal. And right here we encounter a major problem with ritual and sacraments: they attempt a moral rescue of the unseen and nonphysical spirit and soul of man with physical and visible ceremony. That won't work.

SACRAMENTS AND RITUALS CANNOT PAY FOR SIN

This grave error of sacramentalism persists even among a majority of those who call themselves Christians. They imagine that through participation in the visible, and thus temporal, sacrament, they receive invisible and eternal spiritual benefits. Clearly, this is impossible. The Bible declares, "Faith is the substance of things hoped for, the evidence of things not seen" (Hebrews 11:1). Salvation, because it necessarily involves the eternal and invisible, not that which is seen and is therefore temporal, must be by faith, not by physical works or ritual.

Ritual and sacraments have nothing to do with either justice or punishment and therefore cannot possibly pay for sin.

Furthermore, ritual and sacraments have nothing to do with either justice or punishment and therefore cannot possibly pay for sin. One might as well imagine that some ritual could satisfy a court of law in paying the penalty prescribed for a major crime as imagine that God would accept sacraments in payment of the infinite penalty He has prescribed for breaking His law.

The Bible gives two sacraments for the Christian: baptism and communion (also called the Lord's supper). Both are symbolic reminders of a spiritual and eternal transaction that has already taken place: Christ's death, burial, and resurrection, and our identification with Him by faith in His full payment of the penalty for our sins.

Neither baptism nor communion is efficacious. To imagine that they are—and therefore to rely upon either or both of them to effect, even partially, one's salvation—is to reject the salvation God offers in grace to those who believe His promise.

In none of the world's religions is there any concept of God's perfect justice having to be satisfied for the sinner to be forgiven. Instead, works and rituals and mystical experiences are offered to appease God and/or to earn one's salvation. The Bible, however, finds all the world guilty of rebellion against God and insists that human guilt can be forgiven only on a righteous basis. The penalty that God decreed must be paid in full.

GOD'S JUSTICE MUST BE SATISFIED

No one can pay for his own sins, either by sacrifice (even of himself in death) or by good works. Only Christ, who is God and man in one person and who lived without any sin, could pay for the sins of the world. Nor can we merit, earn, or purchase from God—who is perfectly holy and just—the benefit of Christ's sacrifice in forgiveness of our sins. If we are to receive the pardon that Christ has earned, we must receive it by faith as those unworthy of it—the gift of God's grace.

The purpose of the Ten Commandments was not to offer salvation to those who could keep them (no one has ever done so except Christ), but to show us our guilt so that we would accept Christ's payment that satisfied God's justice on our behalf:

> *Wherefore, the law was our schoolmaster to bring us unto Christ, that we might be justified by faith. (Galatians 3:24)*
>
> *Therefore by the deeds of the law there shall no flesh be justified in his sight: for by the law is the knowledge of sin...that every mouth may be stopped, and all the world may become guilty before God.... For God hath concluded them all in unbelief, that he might have mercy upon all.*
>
> *For the wages of sin is death; but the gift of God is eternal life through Jesus Christ our Lord. (Romans 3:19-20; 11:32; 6:23)*

The attempt to offer works or rituals in payment for salvation is true even of some groups who claim to be Christian but who set up their own rules for gaining heaven in opposition to the biblical gospel of salvation by faith and grace alone *without works*. The Bible clearly says, "...that whosoever believeth in him [Christ] should not perish, but have everlasting life" (John 3:16); "For by grace are ye saved through faith...not of works, lest any man should boast" (Ephesians 2:8–9); and "Not by works of righteousness which we have done, but according to his mercy he saved us...that being justified by his grace, we should be made heirs according to the hope of eternal life" (Titus 3:5-7). Any attempt to make even a partial payment for God's gift by His grace is a rejection of that gift.

That good deeds cannot pay for sins is not only biblical but logical. Even a traffic ticket cannot be paid on that basis. It will not avail to ask the judge to dismiss the charge for speeding because the guilty party has driven more often within the speed limit than he has exceeding it. Nor would the judge waive the payment of any crime in response to the defendant's promise never, ever to break the law again. The judge would simply say, "If you never break the law again you are only doing what the law requires. You receive no *extra* credit by which to pay for having broken the law in the past. That penalty is a separate issue and must be paid as prescribed."

That good deeds cannot pay for sins is not only biblical but logical. Even a traffic ticket cannot be paid on that basis...God's justice is infinite and that man, being finite, could never pay the infinite penalty it demands.

The Bible further asserts that God's justice is infinite and that man, being finite, could never pay the infinite penalty it demands. We would be separated from God forever if we tried to work off the debt owed to His justice. God, being infinite, could pay that infinite penalty, but it wouldn't be just, because He is not one of us. Therefore, God became a man through the virgin birth in order to take upon Himself, in our place, the judgment we deserve. And it is *only* on the basis of that penalty having been paid in full that God can justly offer forgiveness.

WHY FAITH IS ESSENTIAL

How amazing that religions that rely upon good works and rituals are considered to be "faiths." Faith can only engage the unseen and eternal and, therefore, does not mix with works and ritual. In search of a valid faith, it is folly to look at that which is visible. Even to look to a visible cross or crucifix is of no merit. What occurred on the cross for our salvation was invisible and must be accepted by faith.

The visible torture Christ endured, the scourging and mocking and nailing to the cross, is not the basis of our salvation.

The visible torture men inflicted upon Christ, the scourging, mocking, and nailing to the cross, is not the basis of our salvation—though that was the message of the popular film *The Passion of the Christ.* There is no virtue in making the "sign of the cross" or waving a cross or crucifix to ward off Satan or evil. It was the judgment Christ endured at the hands of God in payment of the penalty for our sins that makes it possible for God to offer salvation. That suffering, endured by Christ, was totally invisible to man and must ever be. It is by faith alone that we believe Christ paid the penalty and by which we receive the eternal salvation He offers.

The Bible speaks of *"the faith* which was once [for all time] delivered unto the saints" and declares that we must "earnestly contend" for this unchangeable truth because there are false teachers even inside the church who will seek through subterfuge to oppose it (Jude 3–4). Jude is not referring to faith in the sense of believing that a prayer will be answered or an event will occur. "The faith" is the body of truth that must be believed for one to be a Christian.

The Bible allows for no compromise, no discussion, no dialogue with the world's religions (remember, Christianity is not a religion but distinct from all of them) in search for common ground. There is no common ground as far as God, Jesus Christ, and salvation are concerned. The very suggestion that dialogue may be appropriate denies that "the faith" has unique doctrinal content as a definitive body of truth for which we must earnestly contend, and opens the door to compromise in the interest of public relations.

The Bible allows for no compromise, no discussion, no dialogue with the world's religions... Christianity is not a religion but distinct from all of them.

Jesus didn't say, "Go into all the world and dialogue about faith." He said, "Go ye into all the world, and preach the gospel" (Mark 16:15). Paul didn't dialogue with the rabbis and philosophers and pagan priests. He "*disputed* in the synagogue with the Jews, and with the devout persons, and in the market daily" (Acts 17:17). Was it because he was angry and argumentative?

No, because the eternal destiny of his hearers depended upon whether they believed or rejected the gospel.

A reasonable and genuine faith must take very seriously what Jesus said—not what somebody says about what Jesus said, but His very words as recorded in the Bible. And we must face this truth for ourselves, not look to someone else to interpret it for us, no matter what credentials that person or church or institution might claim qualifies them to think for us. We must arrive at this serious faith personally, for true faith is between each individual and God.

7

Prophetic Proof

And now I have told you before it come to pass, that, when it is come to pass, ye might believe.

—John 14:29

Only the Bible has written the details of history centuries and even thousands of years before they happened. It is this fact, above all, that puts the Bible in a class of its own. Its many plainly stated prophecies (not in guarded, ambiguous language like the French quatrains of Nostradamus) were recorded centuries and even thousands of years before their accurate fulfillment. These prophecies are so numerous, stated in perfect agreement by so many different biblical prophets who had no contact with one another, and many of the prophecies so unlikely ever to happen given the normal course of events, that the probability of fulfillment by chance is infinitely remote. Yet they have all been fulfilled with 100 percent accuracy—a fact that cannot be explained away by the skeptics on any rational basis. One is forced from this evidence alone to admit the supernatural origin of the Bible.

There are no prophecies of verifiable date of origin and documented fulfillment centuries later—*not one*—in the Qur'an, in the Hindu Vedas, in the sayings of Buddha, in the sayings of Confucius, or in any other scriptures of the world's religions. The Bible, however, is about 28 percent prophecy, and its thousands of prophecies cover a wide range of subjects and events.

MOST PROPHECY HAS ALREADY BEEN FULFILLED

Some biblical prophecy awaits future fulfillment: the Rapture (the catching up by Christ of all true believers to heaven), the revealing of Antichrist and the establishment of his world government, the Great Tribulation, Armageddon, and the Second Coming of Christ to rescue Israel. Most Bible prophecies, however, have *already* been fulfilled, and these constitute irrefutable proof that the Bible is the inspired Word of God. Repeatedly, the God of the Bible reminds us that He alone declares what will happen in advance and proves that He is the only true God by specific fulfillment of prophecy. For example:

> *Behold, the former things [I foretold through my prophets] are come to pass, and new things do I declare: before they spring forth I tell you of them.*
>
> *I am God, and there is none like me, declaring the end from the beginning, and from ancient times the things that are not yet done, saying, My counsel shall stand, and I will do all my pleasure.*
>
> *I have even from the beginning declared it to thee; before it came to pass I showed it thee: lest thou shouldest say, Mine idol hath done them. (Isaiah 42:9; 46:9–10; 48:5)*

There are two major topics of prophecy in the Bible: Israel and the Messiah who comes to Israel and through Israel to the world. There are hundreds of prophecies concerning Israel (God's chosen people) that have been fulfilled, and many more are in the process of fulfillment, as we are witnessing in our day. The fulfillment of prophecies concerning Israel is found throughout vital parts of history acknowledged by the entire world. Here is a brief outline.

False Claims By "Palestinians"

According to the Bible, God gave the land of Israel exclusively to His chosen people, the Jews. It was specifically promised to the descendants of "Abraham, Isaac, and Jacob" (Genesis 12:7; 13:15; 15:7, 18-21; 17:7-8, 19, 21; 26:3-5; 28:13; Exodus 6:4,8; 1 Chronicles 16:16-18, etc.). Israel was the new name given by God to Jacob, and it is from this name that the Promised Land derives its proper title to this day. The importance of these people can be seen in the fact that God tells Moses, "I am...the God of Abraham, the God of Isaac, and the God of Jacob...this is my name for ever, and this is my memorial unto all generations" (Exodus 3:6,15). The Bible identifies God in this way 12 times, the number of the tribes of Israel. Another 203 times He is called "the God of Israel."

Most Bible prophecies... have already been fulfilled, and these constitute irrefutable proof that the Bible is the inspired Word of God.

Certain Arabs, who only within the last forty years began to call themselves "Palestinians," claim the land of Israel as the surviving descendants of its original inhabitants. That clearly fraudulent assertion is the basis for their intended displacement of Israel and causes the conflict in the Middle East.

These Arabs claim that they are descended from Ishmael, Abraham's first son, and that therefore the Promised Land belongs to them. But Ishmael—even had there been a Palestinian people—was not a Palestinian. His mother was Hagar, the Egyptian maid (Genesis 16:1) of Abraham's wife, Sarah, while Ishmael's father was Abraham, who was from Ur of the Chaldees (Genesis 11:31)—neither of them were Palestinians! When Abraham brought his wife, servants, and flocks into the Promised Land that God gave to him and to his heirs by an everlasting covenant (Genesis 13:15; 17:7, etc.), it was called Canaan and was inhabited by Canaanites (Genesis 12:5-6; 13:7,12, etc.). Arabs who make the impossible claim of descent both from Ishmael and from the original inhabitants of that land are simply lying.

The land of Canaan, to which God brought Abraham, became Israel, a great kingdom of the Jewish people for more than 1,500 years. There was no such place as "Palestine" and no such people as "Palestinians" until the Romans, in anger, in A.D. 135, renamed Israel *Provincia Syria-Palestinia* after her chief enemies the Philistines. Thereafter, its inhabitants were called "Palestinians," an appellation which the Arabs steadfastly refused, insisting that the Jews were the "Palestinians." It was not until the early 1960s that certain Arabs began to claim that they were indeed "Palestinians" and that the Jews were occupying the land they had inherited from ancient ancestors.

On the contrary, God told Abraham specifically that Isaac (his son by Sarah) and his descendants would inherit the Promised Land (Genesis 17:15-21). The earliest verses in the Qur'an support the writings of Moses as true. To escape the honest consequences of that embarrassing fact, Islam claims that the Bible was subsequently corrupted—a claim for which no evidence can be offered. In fact, we have Torah manuscripts both before and after Muhammad, and they are identical. The Qur'an itself declares repeatedly that Allah brought the

Jews out of slavery in Egypt, destroyed Pharaoh's pursuing army, gave Israel the Promised Land, and brought them into it (Surah 5:70; 10:91,94; 17:103-104; 44:30-32; 45:16; 95:20-21, etc.).

FURTHER PROOF SUPPORTING ISRAEL'S LEGITIMACY

Furthermore, God told Abraham that the heirs to the Promised Land would be slaves in a foreign land for 400 years before they took possession of the land He had given to them (Genesis 15:13-16). This happened to the Jews exactly as foretold—not to the Arabs. The Jews became an identifiable ethnic group from isolation as slaves in Egypt for four centuries and were then brought into Canaan. In contrast, the Arabs are not of pure descent from Ishmael but are a mixed race. They settled not in the Promised Land but in the Arabian Peninsula, where they became an identifiable people group. Arabs never came to "Palestine" in any numbers until they invaded it in the seventh century A.D.

Today, only the Jews, and no other people on earth, can legitimately trace their ancestry back to... the Promised Land, and their existence there for centuries as a nation.

Today, only the Jews, and no other people on earth, can legitimately trace their ancestry back to slavery in Egypt, their miraculous deliverance therefrom, their entrance as a unique people group into the Promised Land, and their existence there for centuries as a nation.

As proof that they are the ex-slaves and chosen people, they alone keep the feast of the Passover as a memorial of this event, as God commanded (Exodus 12:14-28)—and have done so each year ever since.

The descendants of Abraham, Isaac, and Jacob, known as "the children of Israel," were led to the Promised Land by Moses nearly 3,500 years ago. At that time, God warned His people through Moses that they would rebel against Him, and because of that, He would scatter them to every part of this world, where they would be hated, persecuted, and slaughtered like no other people (Deuteronomy 4:27; 28:37, 63-64; 2 Chronicles 7:20; Nehemiah 1:8; Jeremiah 15:4; 29:18; 44:8; Amos 9:9; Zechariah 7:14, etc.). And so it happened. Numerous prophets foretold in detail what we now identify as anti-Semitism—that the Jews would be maligned, mistreated, killed, and discriminated against by all other nationalities. At the same time, God promised to preserve the Jews as an identifiable ethnic people and to bring them, in the last days, back into their own land of Israel (Jeremiah 30:7-11; 31:8-12, 27-40; 36, etc.). No non-Jews, whether Arabs or any other nationality, have any claim upon that land, which God has promised to defend.

Nothing about the great events foretold in the Bible concerning Israel is found in the writings of any of the world's religions.

Through the prophet Zechariah (12:1-3), God declared that in the last days preceding Christ's Second Coming, when the Jews had been restored to the Promised Land, Jerusalem would be like a millstone around the necks of the nations. Today, it is the world's major problem; a nuclear war could break out at any time over that Holy City. In remarkable fulfillment of prophecy, the United Nations Security Council has devoted nearly one-third of its deliberations and resolutions to Israel, a country with less than one-thousandth of the earth's population. That would not be the case were it not for the fulfillment of another amazing prophecy: that tiny Israel would be so powerful militarily that she would defeat the surrounding nations that would attack her (Zechariah 12:6-9).

No one can be an honest atheist or agnostic. Prophecy proves the existence of the true God and that the Bible is His Word.

Israel's history is the undeniable unfolding of prophecy fulfilled, exactly as foretold in the Bible—and more is to come. Yet to be fulfilled in the near future are prophecies declaring that Israel will be deceived into making a false peace that will set her up for an attack by all the nations of the world under the leadership of Antichrist. Current events seem to be heading in that direction. That horrible war, which will take the lives of two-thirds of all Jews on earth (Zechariah 13:8-9), will bring the intervention of Jesus Christ from heaven to rescue Israel and to destroy Antichrist and his world government. All indications today are that we are indeed heading toward a world government and Armageddon.

ANTICHRIST AND CHRIST

The Bible declares that Antichrist will control all banking and commerce in the entire world with a number (Revelation 13:16-18), a remarkable prophecy anticipating modern computer technology. Furthermore, Christ declared that if He did not stop Armageddon, no one would be left alive on earth (Matthew 24:22)—another astonishing prophecy that anticipated today's weapons of mass destruction, unknown to past generations.

There are thousands of verses in the Bible dealing with Israel. Prophecies pertaining to Israel are a major part of the Judeo-Christian Scriptures. Yet nothing about the great events foretold in the Bible concerning Israel is found in the writings of any of the world's religions. Nor do they contain any prophecies concerning Israel's Messiah—nor even for any of their founders. There are no verifiable and clear prophecies foretelling the coming of Buddha, Confucius, Muhammad, Zoroaster, the Bab, Baha'ullah, and others in any scriptures.

Paul was not the inventor of Christianity, as some have claimed, nor even was Jesus. Christianity is the fulfillment of hundreds of prophecies.

But for the Jewish Messiah there are literally hundreds of specific prophecies, all of which were undeniably fulfilled in the life, death, and resurrection of Jesus of Nazareth. The Bible prophesied where Christ would be born (Micah 5:2), that He would be betrayed for thirty pieces of silver, which would be thrown down in the temple (Zechariah 11:12-13), and that He would be rejected by His own people (Isaiah 53:2-3). The Bible prophesied the calendar date of the *very day* the Messiah would ride into Jerusalem (Daniel 9:25; Nehemiah 2:1-8), that He would be hailed as the Messiah, although humbly riding into Jerusalem on a donkey (Zechariah 9:9), then crucified four days later (Exodus 12:6; Psalm 22:14-18; Zechariah 12:10–all recorded centuries before crucifixion was practiced on earth), and that He would rise from the dead the third day (Psalm 16:10, Isaiah 53:8-12; Jonah 1:17). Many other details were also prophesied.

No one can be an honest atheist or agnostic. Prophecy proves the existence of the true God and that the Bible is His Word.

No one can be an honest atheist or agnostic. Prophecy proves the existence of the true God and that the Bible is His Word. The fulfillment of numerous prophecies in the life, death, and resurrection of Jesus of Nazareth cannot be explained by coincidence and proves beyond dispute that He is the only Savior of mankind, exactly as He claimed to be. If Jesus did not fulfill, without exception, what the Hebrew prophets declared in the Scriptures concerning the coming of the promised Messiah, then no matter how appealing we may find His teaching and personality, He would have to be rejected.

The Conversion of Gentiles Foretold

Furthermore, that millions of non-Jews all over the world would become believers in the God of Israel, and that this would happen through their faith in the very Messiah whom the Jews would reject, was prophesied repeatedly by Hebrew prophets throughout the Old Testament (Genesis 12:3; Psalm 22:27; Isaiah 52:10; Malachi 1:11, etc.). The rabbis and even Christ's disciples did not recognize these prophecies, not because the language was unclear, but because they were blinded by unbelief. That the conversion of hundreds of millions of Gentiles has happened in spite of the unbelief of the Jewish nation in their Messiah is one of the most remarkable developments in history. Today, there are about two billion people who, though they are not all true Christians according to the standards Jesus set, claim to believe in Him and, through Him, to believe in the God of Abraham, Isaac, and Jacob.

Paul was not the inventor of Christianity, as some have claimed, nor even was Jesus. Christianity is the fulfillment of hundreds of prophecies.

Paul was not the inventor of Christianity, as some have claimed, nor even was Jesus. Christianity is the fulfillment of hundreds of prophecies. Not only that there would be multitudes of Gentile believers, but also the specifics of the doctrines of salvation were laid out clearly in the Old Testament. Christ himself pointed to these prophecies, and Paul made them the basis of the gospel he preached (1 Corinthians 15:1-4, etc.). This is absolutely unique. There is no comparable verification for any of the doctrines of any of the world's religions.

PROPHETIC PROOF OF THE BIBLE

Paul declared that "the gospel of God" that he preached was backed up by the Old Testament. He begins his epistle to the Romans with these words: "Paul, a servant of Jesus Christ, called to be an apostle, separated unto the gospel of God (which he had promised afore by his prophets in the holy scriptures)" (Romans 1:1–2). In every city Paul entered on his missionary journeys, he went first of all into the synagogue and proved to the Jewish congregants that what their own prophets had foretold concerning the coming Messiah, Jesus Christ had fulfilled, including His death on the cross and His resurrection: "And Paul, as his manner was, went in unto them [in the synagogue], and three sabbath days reasoned with them out of the [Hebrew] scriptures, opening and alleging, that Christ must needs have suffered, and risen again from the dead; and that this Jesus, whom I preach unto you, is Christ" (Acts 17:2–3).

It would be folly to step into eternity trusting (in rejection of God's Word) one's own ideas, or the ideas of some church or religious leader.

Christ did exactly the same. He scolded the two disheartened disciples, who knew the tomb was empty but didn't believe that Christ had risen from the dead, as they were walking to Emmaus from Jerusalem three days after His crucifixion. He said: "O fools, and slow of heart to believe all that the prophets have spoken: ought not Christ to have suffered these things [i.e., rejection by Israel and crucifixion], and to enter into his glory? And beginning at Moses and all the prophets, he expounded unto them in all the scriptures the things concerning himself" (Luke 24:25-27). He told His disciples repeatedly that "all things must be fulfilled, which were written in the law of Moses, and in the prophets, and in the psalms, concerning me" (Luke 24:44).

To whatever extent one relies upon some third party (pastor, priest, preacher, author, church, etc.) to interpret the Bible, to that extent one has lost contact with God and His Word.

It would be folly to step into eternity trusting (in rejection of God's Word) one's own ideas or the ideas of some church or religious leader. All who would know their eternal destiny for certain must rely upon what the Bible itself proves to be true about salvation and living the Christian life. Because of the irrefutable proof that it is God's Word, the Bible must be our authority.

We commend the Bible to each reader. Do not take our word, but search God's Word for yourself. Why is this personal study necessary? Because to whatever extent one relies upon some third party (pastor, priest, preacher, author, church, etc.) to interpret the Bible, to that extent one has lost contact with God and His Word. God wants to speak to each individual through His Word and through Jesus Christ, not through some intermediary.

In our earnest desire to know the one true God, we must turn to the Scriptures alone.

The Bible itself says, "Faith cometh by hearing...the word of God" (Romans 10:17). In our earnest desire to know the one true God, we must turn to the Scriptures alone. It is up to each one to check it all out from there, the only infallible authority and, having examined the proofs, to believe the Word of God. Such is the basis of true faith—the only faith that saves for eternity.

8

Concerning Prayer

But as for me, my prayer is unto thee,
O Lord...

—Psalm 69:13

The major partner to faith is prayer. Most people (religious or not, and even professing atheists), when desperate enough, have devoted at least some time and effort to prayer. Generally, prayer is thought to be a religious technique for talking some "god" or "higher power" into giving the petitioner what he or she wants. Few indeed are those who truly know God and sincerely pray, "Not my will but Thine be done." That attitude, however, necessarily belongs to those who by faith are confident that God truly loves them, is wiser than they are, and therefore desire His will, confident that it would be infinitely better than their own.

In attempting to use prayer to get their own way, those who pray (including many who call themselves Christians) try very hard to drum up "faith," imagining that the key to answered prayer is to somehow *believe* the answer will come. If, however, believing strongly enough that something will occur causes it to happen, then one doesn't need God. One could, by simply believing, bring into existence whatever one wanted without regard to any god.

"FAITH" IN POSITIVE THINKING

And if that can be done, why bother with prayer at all? Why not simply affirm repeatedly what one desires? In fact, that is exactly what many people do, even those who are not at all religious. Positive affirmations play a large part in motivational and success seminars in the business world. If those who follow this practice, however, are willing to be honest with themselves, they must admit that this method is largely unsuccessful—for which we should all be thankful. How frightening it would be, and what chaos would reign, if everyone had the power to impose his or her will on the universe and upon the rest of mankind by affirming personal desires.

It is irrational to believe that affirmations will cause anything to occur in the real world.

It is irrational to believe that affirmations will cause anything to occur in the real world. What is the mechanism or universal law by which someone's belief or affirmation controls the course of events? The power of one's own mind? The desire for which one prays or makes affirmations to bend events to one's will almost inevitably involves factors that affect other people's lives. Why should one person's desires be imposed upon others? And what god or force would so readily accommodate individual passions?

What chaos would reign, if everyone had the power to impose his or her will on the universe and upon the rest of mankind by affirming personal desires.

Suppose several firmly held beliefs and affirmations of different individuals are in direct conflict with one another, as many of them inevitably must be. What then? Which one will this universal mechanism or law cause to occur? And, indeed, how can a mechanism or law decide anything? In fact, an impersonal force or principle cannot make choices or distinctions, so every affirmation would have to be granted.

Here we see a major problem with this theory: if unlimited power were made available to everyone, the result would not be peace and blessing but increased conflict between human egos, resulting in even greater chaos than before. Surely, if answers to prayer are to come, one would hope that a Supreme Intelligence that is just and impartial is in charge of the process.

TRUE FAITH MUST BE IN GOD

Jesus said, "Have faith in God" (Mark 11:22). Does that mean that the God revealed in the Bible exists as our servant to give us what we want? On the contrary, He is not a cosmic bellhop or a genie in a bottle to grant wishes upon demand, though that is the only god in whom many are willing to believe. Faith is not a force we aim at God to get Him to bend to our will and cater to our wants. According to Jesus, the object of faith must be the one true God and His truth. Prayer is petitioning God and must therefore be subject to His will, or else it would be rebellion.

Faith is not a force we aim at God to get Him to bend to our will and cater to our wants.

Faith is not managing to believe that *somehow* one's prayer will be answered. That would be mind power. Faith is believing that *God* will grant one's request. That fact changes everything. What we are praying for may not be God's will, God's way, or in God's time. There is a huge difference between trying to influence God to grant what we desire and trusting Him to give us what He knows we need. Scripture declares: "Ye ask, and receive not, because ye ask amiss, that ye may consume it upon your lusts" (James 4:3).

The implication is that God refuses to grant requests for self-gratification. Prayer is not a technique for getting one's own way. Rather it is an appeal to the Creator who is still in charge of His universe. But can't He be persuaded? God does reward earnestness. We are told to persist in prayer, no doubt to develop our character rather than to persuade Him. Would we really want to persuade God to bend His will to ours? It is right here that much misunderstanding about prayer causes so many to be disappointed or even disillusioned.

IS "IN JESUS' NAME" AN "OPEN SESAME"?

Jesus said, "Whatsoever ye shall ask the Father in my name, he will give it you" (John 16:23). Is this like "Open Sesame"? Obviously, to ask in Christ's name must mean more than just speaking out His name like a magic password for getting what we want. The ambassador who represents the United States in a foreign country has the right to use America's name and authority but not for his own ends. The business manager representing a multimillionaire has power of attorney that gives him the right to use his employer's name, even to sign contracts and large checks. However, any use of the other's name is to be in the interest and for the benefit of that one, not for the benefit of his subordinate agent.

Prayer is petitioning God and must therefore be subject to His will, or else it would be rebellion.

It would be fraud for the employee to enrich himself through the use of his employer's name. Yet would-be

Christians by the millions imagine that they can use the name of Jesus to their own ends. To ask in the name of Jesus is to ask as Jesus would ask, in fulfillment of the Father's will and to His glory. Who would want it otherwise, except an egomaniac so ignorant of his own selfishness and folly as to imagine that he could manage the universe better than God!

Faith itself is a gift from God, which He bestows on those who desire to know and do His will.

Of course, the God whom we petition cannot be a stranger (it would be folly to trust a stranger) or One from whom we are alienated. He must be One whom we know and with whom we have a right relationship. True faith, as Jesus taught it, comes from knowing God and trusting Him. Indeed, faith itself is a gift from God, which He bestows on those who desire to know and do His will. To seek an answer to prayer that is contrary to God's will would be rank rebellion.

Still, the idea persists that faith is believing something strongly enough to make it happen. This delusion is usually found among those who imagine they hold to a scientific religion. Science works according to consistent laws. It is commonly taught, especially by those in the so-called faith movement, that there is a "law of faith" that works like gravity or thermodynamics, and if we obey that law, what we desire will be granted as automatically as the predictable reaction between chemicals in a test tube. "Faith" is thus seen as a force we can wield to get what we want rather than a trust in God to effect what is best according to His will. There is a great difference.

This self-centered belief has at least four problems:

1. *The Christian is "not under the law, but under grace" (Romans 6:14), yet grace has no part to play in this supposed law of faith;*

2. *The Bible never even hints that the realm of the spirit is governed by laws similar to those governing the physical realm;*

3. *The physical laws God has established are intended to* **control** *man (even Adam and Eve were subject to them) and to* **limit** *what we can do with God's universe, but this presumed law of faith does just the opposite. It allows each person to become a "god" waving a magic wand over the physical universe—and thus does not fit the pattern of physical laws that God has established; and*

4. *The very heart of the prayer pattern Jesus taught His disciples is, "Thy kingdom come. Thy will be done, in earth as it is in heaven" (Matthew 6:10), but the imagined "law of faith" would accomplish just the opposite, gaining for man the desires of his own will. Indeed, the teachers in this movement insist that it destroys faith to pray "if it be thy [God's] will."*

New Thought, New Age

Very similar to the faith movement within charismatic and Pentecostal circles is the New Thought Alliance of churches. Although they are far outside biblical Christianity, most claim to be Christian, and many of their teachings are similar to those of the faith movement. Popular groups involved include Christian Science, Religious Science, Science of Mind, and Unity, as well as many independent churches not directly affiliated with any of these. And how do they think their affirmations turn into reality? They propose an all-powerful universal Mind that exists to serve mankind. Oddly, this great Mind apparently has no mind of its own but is ever ready to turn wishes into horses so everyone can ride who knows how to tap into this ever-available power. Only the human ego, deluded by Satan's "I will be like the most High" (Isaiah 14:14), could persist in such an egotistic concept.

Hinduism holds to a similar belief. It denies objective reality and claims that we have created with our minds an imaginary universe called *maya*. By changing our thinking, we can change our universe. One sees bumper stickers that apparently reflect the same superstition: "Think Snow," or "Visualize Peace." And at least some of those who display these slogans actually believe that the united thinking of enough people can literally create snow or peace or anything else that is desired.

Positive Mental Attitude (PMA) seminars and much success training in the business world involve a similar fantasy—the idea that we can create success by holding positive thoughts of success in our minds. The same is true of the teaching of Positive Thinking and Possibility Thinking, which have gained a wide following among professing Christians and even among evangelicals. According to their chief proponents, Positive Thinking and Possibility Thinking are actually synonymous with faith. On the contrary, atheists can and do teach Positive/Possibility Thinking seminars. No atheist, however, can have biblical faith, which is *in God.* Nor has the Creator, thankfully, put His universe and our lives at the mercy of our badly flawed "positive" thinking.

True faith is absolute, unquestioning trust in God and in His love, wisdom, and will.

Trusting God

True faith is absolute, unquestioning trust in God and in His love, wisdom, and will. Nor is such total trust foreign to man. It is a necessity. Trusting in another's wisdom, ability, and integrity is something that all of us, whether atheist, agnostic, or religionist, must do many times each day. We go to a doctor, who makes a diagnosis that we couldn't understand even if he explained it. He writes out a prescription in a hand we can't decipher and couldn't comprehend even if we could read it. We take that to a pharmacist, who puts together compounds with mysterious names totally foreign to our understanding. Yet we ingest the medicine because we trust our doctor and pharmacist for the promised results. In fact, we must trust them in order to benefit from an expertise that we lack.

We don't force our way into the cockpit of the commercial aircraft in which we're flying to look over the pilots' shoulders to make certain they are doing their job. We don't know how to fly that aircraft, and we have no choice but to trust the flying to them. Nor do we look over the mechanic's shoulder as he tunes our engine, or stay up all night to make certain that the baker puts the right ingredients into the bread we'll purchase the next day. Clearly, in the progress of daily affairs, we must constantly rely upon experts who know what we don't know and can do what we can't do.

The gravest error associated with prayer is to imagine that it is essential for salvation.

Such trust is essential, because we can't know everything we need to know to be even moderately successful in life on this earth, much less to surmount every difficulty and solve every problem we will face in our threescore years and ten. Unfortunately, all of us at times have been hurt one way or another by reliance upon a supposed expert who made a costly mistake either because he or she was incompetent or was only human, and to err is human. Fortunately, no matter how serious such mishaps may be, we can usually recover—though often with great cost and difficulty and only after much time. When it comes to eternal matters, however, such recovery is not possible once we have passed through death's door.

THE FAITH THAT SAVES

There are many self-professed "experts" in spiritual matters. They claim to know about heaven and hell but have never been there. They generally offer weak reasons for trusting them: they have degrees from a seminary; they've been ordained by some religious body; they've been voted into a position of authority by a committee; they've written some books; their denomination is the oldest or largest; their church is the only correct one and outside of it there is no salvation; they are apostles or prophets and get continuing revelations from God, and so on. None of these reasons can be the basis of true faith. Where is the evidence that they should be believed and that we should therefore follow them into eternity? We dare not take that trip without absolute certainty.

The gravest error associated with prayer is to imagine that it is essential for salvation. On the contrary, as we have seen from the Scriptures (which alone deserve our trust), God offers salvation as a free gift. When a gift is offered, one does not beg for it, plead for it, or agonize for it. One simply receives it. To beg or plead or pray for the gift is to betray one's lack of faith in the giver and his offer.

In order to get serious about faith, one must realize that faith is not a magic wand we wave to get what we want. Far from having some power within itself, faith must have an object. There are two essential ingredients in faith: *what* one believes and *in whom* one believes.

Faith can either fulfill or disappoint. Remember, faith is in the invisible and eternal and thus determines one's eternal destiny. Obviously, to believe what is false about eternity and the God of eternity is to set oneself up for eternal loss and remorse.

No tragedy could be greater.

9

What Is the Gospel?

Go ye into all the world, and preach the gospel...for it is the power of God unto salvation to every one that believeth [it].

—Mark 16:15; Romans 1:16

What is the gospel that saves—and from what does it save us? In order to answer that question, we must go back to the Garden of Eden. It was there, in the most perfect environment that God's heart of love and His creative power could provide, that man's rebellion against his Creator had its awful beginning. Eden is not mythology but history, as human experience, selfish ambition, and false religions continue to demonstrate to the present day.

Surrounded by beauty, satisfied by abundance, and enjoying the fellowship of their Infinite Friend, our first parents, nevertheless, fell to the seductive lies of Satan. "Ye shall be as gods" was his deceitful promise—and to realize that delusion has been man's passion ever since. False religions, such as Hinduism and Mormonism, are based upon this lie.

Though not deceived himself (1 Timothy 2:14), Adam, in loyalty to Eve, joined in his wife's disobedience and ate of the forbidden fruit. Thus, "by [this] one man sin entered into the world, and death by sin; and so death passed upon all men, for that all have sinned" (Romans 5:12).

A Planned Salvation

Death not only ends this short earthly life, it separates sinful rebels from God forever. In His infinite foreknowledge, wisdom, and love, however, God had already planned how He would restore life and reunite mankind with Himself. Without ceasing to be God, He would become a man through a virgin birth. Only God could be the Savior (Isaiah 43:11; 45:21); thus the Messiah had to be God (Isaiah 9:6; 45:15; Titus 1:3,4). He would die for our sins to pay the penalty demanded by His own perfect justice: "'Tis mystery all, the *Immortal* dies!" hymn writer Charles Wesley declared. Then He would rise from the dead to live in those who would believe in and receive Him as their Lord and Savior. Forgiveness of sins and eternal life would be theirs as a free gift of His grace—the only way man could receive it.

Centuries before His incarnation as the perfect man, Christ Jesus, God inspired the Old Testament prophets to declare His eternal and unchangeable plan of salvation. Definitive criteria were provided by which the coming Savior would be identified. Jesus and His apostles did not invent a "new religion." Christianity fulfills scores of specific prophecies and is therefore provable from Old Testament Hebrew Scripture!

Salvation comes on God's terms...we negotiate the gospel neither with God nor with one another.

So it was not a new gospel that Paul the apostle preached. It was "the gospel of God (which he had promised afore by his prophets in the holy scriptures) concerning his Son Jesus Christ" (Romans 1:1-3). Thus, the Bereans could check Paul's message against the Old Testament (Acts 17:11); and he could use the Hebrew prophets, which were read in the synagogue each Sabbath, to prove that Jesus was the promised Messiah (verses 2–3). Not Buddha, not Muhammad, not anyone else—only Jesus Christ has the required credentials. The fulfillment of scores of specific prophecies in the life, death, and resurrection of Jesus of Nazareth provides absolute proof that He is the true and only Savior.

THE ONLY ESCAPE FROM GOD'S JUDGMENT

In Hebrews 2:3 the vital question is asked, "How shall we escape, if we neglect so great salvation?" The answer is unequivocal: there is no escape for those who reject Christ. The Bible makes that solemn fact abundantly clear. To reject, add to, take from, or otherwise pervert or embrace a substitute for "the gospel of God" is to perpetuate the rebellion begun by Adam and Eve and to leave one eternally separated from God and His proffered salvation.

No wonder Paul wrote, "Knowing therefore the terror of the Lord, we persuade men" (2 Corinthians 5:11). So must all who know Christ persuade men to believe the only gospel that saves! We do this not for any credit or reward, much less to get others to "join our side," but out of love and compassion for all mankind—the same love that God manifested in providing salvation for sinners and that He has implanted in the hearts of all true believers.

The "gospel of your salvation" (Ephesians 1:13) "wherein ye stand; by which also ye are saved" (1 Corinthians 15:1–2) is simple and precise, leaving no room for misunderstanding or negotiation: "that Christ died for our sins according to the scriptures; and that he was buried, and that he rose again the third day according to the scriptures" (verses 3–4).

This "everlasting gospel" (Revelation 14:6) was promised "before the world began" (2 Timothy 1:9; Titus 1:2) and cannot change with time or culture. There is no other hope for mankind, no other way to be forgiven and brought back to God, except through this "strait gate and narrow way" (Matthew 7:13–14). Any broader road leads to destruction according to Jesus himself.

The one true "gospel of God's grace," which God offers as our *only* salvation, has three basic elements: 1) who Christ is—fully God and perfect, sinless man in one Person (were He less, He could not be our Savior), 2) who we are—hopeless sinners already condemned to eternal death (or we wouldn't need to be saved), and 3) what Christ's death accomplished—the payment of the full penalty for our sins (any attempt by us to pay *in any way* or *any part* demeans what Christ accomplished and rejects the gift of salvation God offers).

ONLY BELIEVE!

Christ has commanded us to "preach the gospel [good news!] to every creature [person]" (Mark 16:15). What response is required? Both the desperate question and uncomplicated answer are given to us: "What must I do to be saved?... *Believe* on the Lord Jesus Christ, and thou shalt be saved" (Acts 16:30–31). Neither religion, ritual, nor good works will avail—God calls us to simply *believe*. "For by grace are ye saved through *faith*" (Ephesians 2:8)— "whosoever *believeth* in him [will] not perish, but [has] everlasting life" (John 3:16).

It is the gospel alone that saves those who believe it. Nothing else will save. Therefore, we must preach the gospel. Paul said, "Woe is unto me, if I preach not the

(1 Corinthians 9:16). Sentimental appeals to "come to Jesus" or "make a decision for Christ" avail nothing if the gospel is not clearly explained and believed.

Many are attracted to Christ because of His admirable character, His noble martyrdom, or because He changes lives. If that is all they see in Christ, such converts have not believed the *gospel* and thus are not saved. This is the solemn teaching of Scripture (John 3:36).

> **We negotiate the gospel neither with God nor with one another...we either believe it or reject it.**

Paul said that "the gospel of Christ...is the power of God *unto salvation* to every one that believeth" (Romans 1:16). He also called it "the gospel...by which also *ye are saved*" (1 Corinthians 15:1–2); and "the gospel of *your salvation*" (Ephesians 1:13). Clearly, from these and other scriptures, salvation comes *only* through *believing the gospel.* Christ told His disciples to go into "all the world, and preach the gospel" (Mark 16:15), a gospel that the Bible precisely defines.

THE NON-NEGOTIABLE GOSPEL

Salvation comes on God's terms and by His grace, and we negotiate the gospel neither with God nor with one another. "The Father sent the Son to be the Saviour of the world" (1 John 4:14). Salvation is a work of God and His Son. We either believe it or reject it. We don't "dialogue" about it. Nor does any church or religious organization have a franchise for dispensing it. Salvation is free from God without any "middleman." It is granted to "whosoever" will take God at His word and accept His pardon by faith.

It is also called the "gospel of Christ" (Mark 1:1; Romans 1:16; 15:19; 1 Corinthians 9:12). He is the Savior and salvation is His work, not ours, as the angels said: "For unto you is born this day in the city of David a Saviour, which is Christ the Lord" (Luke 2:11). Salvation could be accomplished only by Christ, and when He had paid the full penalty by suffering on the Cross for our sins, he cried in triumph, "It is finished" (John 19:30).

The gospel contains nothing about baptism, church membership or attendance, tithing, sacraments or rituals, diet or clothing.

Paul specifies the gospel that saves: "that Christ died for our sins according to the scriptures; and that he was buried, and that he rose again the third day according to the scriptures" (1 Corinthians 15:3–4). "I am the door," said Christ: "By *me* if any man enter in, he shall be saved" (John 10:9).

The gospel contains nothing about baptism, church membership or attendance, tithing, sacraments or rituals, diet or clothing. If we add *anything* to the gospel, we have not only declared it to be insufficient but have corrupted it and thus come under Paul's anathema in Galatians 1:8,9.

The gospel is all about what Christ has done. It says nothing about what Christ must yet do, because the work of our redemption is finished. "Christ *died* for our sins" (1 Corinthians 15:3). His death on the cross is in the past, never to be repeated.

Nor does the gospel say anything about what *we* must do, because we can do nothing. "Not by works of righteousness which we have done, but according to his mercy he saved us" (Titus 3:5); "for by grace are ye saved, through faith...the gift of God [is] not of works, lest any man should boast" (Ephesians 2:8–9). Whoever offers God *anything* for salvation has denied the sufficiency of what Christ did and has rejected God's salvation.

Instead of works, the gospel requires faith. It is the power of God unto salvation to those who *believe.* "But to him that *worketh not,* but *believeth* on him that justifieth the ungodly, his *faith* is counted for righteousness" (Romans 4:5)... "that whosoever believeth in him should not perish, but have everlasting life" (John 3:16).

The gospel is a two-edged sword. It declares, "He that believeth on the Son hath everlasting life." The same verse also says, "he that believeth not the Son shall not see life; but the wrath of God abideth on him" (John 3:36).

ETERNAL PUNISHMENT

Right here we come to the most difficult part of the gospel to accept: that those who do not believe it are eternally lost—no matter what good works they do.

The reasons for that fact are grounded in both God's love and His justice. God's justice requires that the infinite penalty for sin must be paid. For us to pay would separate us from God forever, so He became a man through the virgin birth to pay the penalty for us. No one can complain against God. He has proved His love by doing all He could for our salvation. He has Himself paid the penalty and on that basis can be both "just, and the justifier of him which believeth in Jesus" (Romans 3:26).

Contrary to the message of Mel Gibson's *The Passion of the Christ* there was no payment for sins' penalty in the torture that men inflicted upon the Lord.

Christ pleaded in the Garden, "If it be possible [that is, if there is any other way mankind can be saved], let this cup pass from me" (Matthew 26:39). We know that there is no other way, or God would not have required His beloved Son to bear the full brunt of His wrath against sin. That men nailed Christ to the cross is not the basis of our salvation. That heinous act, perpetrated by men, would only add to our condemnation.

Contrary to the message of Mel Gibson's *The Passion of the Christ*, there was no payment for sins' penalty in the torture that men inflicted upon the Lord. The idea that the godless Roman soldiers were God's servants meting out His punishment for sin upon Christ contradicts both the Scripture and common sense. Did they smite Christ just enough times and just hard enough to punish Him for the sins all mankind, as the movie implies? They punished Christ for the sins of billions of people from the beginning to the end of time? Impossible! It was, in fact, the evil in their hearts that caused the soldiers to abuse Him as they did. And that, too, was sin for which Christ died.

Here, displayed before the universe for all time and eternity, was the greatest proof of the evil in each and every one of us—the creature taunting, torturing, and crucifying its Creator! But when man was doing his worst against Him, God did His best to man in the greatest possible demonstration of His love, grace, and mercy. In response to Christ's incredible cry, "Father, forgive them; for they know not what they do" (Luke 23:34), God punished Him for the sins of the world.

Our salvation was procured not by what His tormentors did but by Christ taking upon Himself "the sin of the world" (John 1:29) and suffering the eternal death ("that he by the grace of God should taste death for every man" –Hebrews 2:9) in the separation from God ("My God, my God, why hast thou forsaken me?" —Matthew 27:46) that all mankind deserved. As the great Hebrew prophet foretold: "The LORD hath laid on him the iniquity of us all.... It pleased the LORD to bruise him; he hath put him to grief: when thou shalt make his soul an offering for sin..." (Isaiah 53:6, 10).

THE PENALTY PAID IN FULL

What happened in those hours of darkness as Christ hung upon the Cross will never be known by mankind. The suffering He endured as all the "waves and billows" (Psalm 42:7) of God's wrath swept over Him is beyond our comprehension. In the face of the most despicable display of the evil in the human heart, when man was doing his worst to his Creator, Christ took all our sins upon Himself and paid the penalty in full.

Christ did not gradually expire from the physical effects of the torture and crucifixion. He had said, "I lay down my life, that I might take it again. No man taketh it from me, but I lay it down of myself. I have power to lay it down, and I have power to take it again" (John 10:17-18). When He had endured God's full judgment for our sins, He who is God cried "with a loud voice" (Matthew 27:50; Mark 15:37; Luke 23:46), "It is finished" (John 19:30). The Greek word He shouted in triumph was *tetelestai*. That word was stamped on promissory notes and invoices in Christ's day. It meant "paid in full."

Christ did not gradually expire from the physical effects of the torture and crucifixion. He had said, "I lay down my life, that I might take it again..."

Only if we accept that payment on our behalf can we be saved. "There is none other name under heaven given among men, whereby we *must* be saved" (Acts 4:12); "What *must* I do to be saved?...Believe on the Lord Jesus

Christ, and thou shalt be saved" (Acts 16:30,31).

To "believe on the Lord Jesus Christ" includes believing *who He is* and *what He has done.* Jesus said, "Ye are from beneath; I am from above...if ye believe not that *I am*...[I AM is God's name, Yahweh –Exodus 3:14], ye shall die in your sins" (John 8:23–24). Jesus himself says we must believe that He is God, for He is; and no one less than God could save us. We must believe that the sinless One "died for our sins," was buried, and rose bodily from the grave. Only by believing this gospel are we saved. So says God's Word.

Evangelistic appeals to "come to Christ" are often made for the wrong reasons...Christ died to rescue us from the penalty of sin, not to make us successful.

But wouldn't the exceptional good works of a Mother Teresa get her to heaven? No, because we are all sinners, including Mother Teresa. Once we have broken one of God's commandments, we are "guilty of all" (James 2:10). Furthermore, "by the deeds of the law there shall no flesh be justified in his sight" (Romans 3:20). Keeping the law perfectly from now on could never make up for having already broken it. Good works, no matter *how* good, can never pay for sin.

For God to grant salvation by any other means than faith in Christ alone would be an insult to the One who the Father insisted had to endure His wrath as the sacrifice for sin. Moreover, if He allowed entrance into heaven on any other basis, God would be breaking His own code of justice and going back on His Word. Not even God himself could gratuitously forgive earth's most notable "saint" without the penalty being paid and accepted by the sinner in gratitude. Christ's blood avails only for repentant sinners.

PERVERTING THE GOSPEL

Oswald Chambers warned lest, in our zeal to get people to accept the gospel, we manufacture a gospel acceptable to people and produce "converts" who are not saved. Today's most popular perversion is the "positive" gospel, which is designed to offend no one with truth. One of our most popular televangelists, for example, has said that it is demeaning to call anyone a sinner and that Christ died to restore human dignity and self-esteem. This televangelist claims to win many to Christ with that seductive message—but such a gospel does not save sinners.

Evangelistic appeals to "come to Christ" are often made for the wrong reasons: in order to be healthy, happy, or successful; to restore a marriage; or to handle stress. Christ died to rescue us from the penalty of sin, not to make us successful. Those who do not admit that they desperately need God's forgiveness in Christ, and thus do not accept His salvation, are not saved but lost eternally.

Others preach a gospel that is so diluted or perverted that it deceives many into thinking they are saved, when in fact they are not. No fraud could be worse, for the consequences are eternal!

Religion, not atheism, is Satan's main weapon. "The god of this world hath blinded the minds of them which believe not, lest the light of the glorious gospel of Christ...should shine unto them" (2 Corinthians 4:4). To pervert "the gospel of the grace of God" (Acts 20:24), the great deceiver offers many false gospels, but they all, as we have seen, have two subtle rejections of grace in common: ritual and/or self-effort.

Ritual makes redemption an ongoing process (unfinished by Christ) performed by a special priesthood, and self-effort gives man a part to play in earning his salvation. The one denies the finality of the cross; the other denies its sufficiency. Either one robs God of the uniqueness of the gift He wishes to bestow upon fallen man: "The wages of sin is death; but the gift of God is eternal life through Jesus Christ our Lord" (Romans 6:23).

Religion, not atheism, is Satan's main weapon.... To look to a church, organization, or some religious leader to dispense God's gift is to reject it from His hand.

One can only *receive* a gift. Any attempt to earn, merit, or pay for a gift, even in part, is to reject it. Furthermore, God wants to personally give us this gift of eternal life through Jesus Christ. To look to a church, organization, or some religious leader to dispense God's gift is to reject it from His hand. Jesus said, "Come unto *me*…*I* give [my sheep] eternal life…*I* am the door; by *me* if any man enter in, he shall be saved…" (Matthew 11:28; John 10:9, 27–28).

Faith must be in God and in Christ alone. To place it anywhere else is to admit a lack of faith in Him. Let us get serious about faith by believing what God has said. Therein lies our only authority and assurance.

10

MERCY VS. WORKS

An altar of earth thou shalt make unto me...And if thou wilt make me an altar of stone, thou shalt not build it of hewn stone: for if thou lift up thy tool upon it, thou hast polluted it. Neither shalt thou go up by steps unto mine altar, that thy nakedness be not discovered thereon.

—EXODUS 20:24-26

Let us build us a city and a tower [of Babel], whose top may reach unto heaven.

—GENESIS 11:4

NO TWO TENETS OF FAITH could be more opposed to one another than those presented above.

Nothing could be clearer than God's rejection of any human effort to buy salvation or His favor. If man is to be accepted by God, it must be solely by God's grace and provision, not by any human work. Man's self-effort and self-righteousness are utterly rejected by God.

Yet in defiance we see man's flagrant repudiation of God's prohibition against self-effort and his arrogant attempt to build a tower that would enable him to climb by steps of his own making into heaven itself. At Babel we meet the first attempt at a world government united with a world religion. Church and state were one: "Go to, let us build us a city [government] and a tower [religion] whose top may reach unto heaven" (Genesis 11:4). It was rebellion in the highest form, and will be realized again under Antichrist.

God's instructions for worshiping Him were explicit. If the ground was too rocky to gather up a mound of earth for an altar, stones could be heaped together—but they could not be cut, fashioned, or polished with a tool. Nor could the altar be elevated. Not one step must be climbed to reach it. There must be no illusion that man could contribute anything by his own efforts to his salvation.

God himself is the only One who can save man, and salvation can only be a gift of His grace. Such is the gospel consistently preached from Genesis to Revelation. Consider the following:

> *I, even I, am the Lord; and beside me there is no saviour. (Isaiah 43:11)*
>
> *For unto us a child [the Messiah] is born... [He is] the mighty God, the everlasting Father. (Isaiah 9:6)*

Thou shalt call his name Jesus: for he shall save his people from their sins. (Matthew 1:21)

They that are in the flesh cannot please God. (Romans 8:8)

For by grace are ye saved…not of works, lest any man should boast. (Ephesians 2:8–9)

Not by works of righteousness which we have done, but according to his mercy he saved us. (Titus 3:5)

Being justified freely by his grace through the redemption that is in Christ Jesus. (Romans 3:24)

And if by grace, then is it no more of works: otherwise grace is no more grace. But if it be of works, then is it no more grace: otherwise work is no more work. (Romans 11:6)

REBELLION TAKES MANY FORMS

It was the incredible act of rebellion in Eden against the Almighty that separated man from his Creator. No less astonishing is the fact that man continues his defiance in his very attempts to be reconciled to God, and so persists in his self-righteous resolve to contribute something toward his salvation.

Thus, amazingly, man's rebellion against God is seen most clearly in his religions, all of which are but mirror images of Babel—ingenious and persistent attempts to "climb up some other way" instead of entering through the door that God has provided in His Son (John 10:9).

Babel may be traced through ancient paganism

to the "high places" (elevated altars) of heathen worship adopted by Israel (Leviticus 26:30; 1 Kings 11:7; 2 Kings 23:15; Ezekiel 16:24-39) and to every religion on earth today. The ornate temples, mosques, and elaborate ceremonies found in Islam, Hinduism, Buddhism, Mormonism, and other cults and the occult are obvious continuations of Babel. So are the magnificent cathedrals, lofty steeples, elevated and gilded altars, luxurious vestments, and impressive rituals of some of today's churches, whether Protestant, Roman Catholic, or Orthodox.

The belief that liturgy's form and formulas transmit spiritual power...too readily creeps into even Protestant thinking.

Such pomp turns off many non-Christians, who rightly want nothing to do with a God who is influenced by ceremonies and fleshly enhancements.

Was not Solomon's temple most magnificent? Yes, but it was uniquely designed and commanded by God. Both the tabernacle in the wilderness and the temple that succeeded it were "a figure [picture]...of good things to come [that is, of Christ and heaven]" (Hebrews 9:9-11). God said to Moses, "See...that thou make all things according to the pattern showed to thee in the mount [Sinai]" (Hebrews 8:5).

No such pattern or approval was given by God for any other religious structure. While Protestants reject relics, statues, and icons, they often refer to their places of worship as "sanctuaries," as though God dwells there. In fact, God inhabits the Christian's body ("your body is the temple of the Holy Ghost"—1 Corinthians 6:19), which is therefore to be kept holy. Paul reminded the Athenians:

> God that made the world and all things therein, seeing that he is Lord of heaven and earth, dwelleth not in temples made with hands; neither is worshipped with men's hands, as though he needed any thing, seeing he giveth to all life, and breath, and all things. (Acts 17:24–25)

GRACE IS "IN SPITE," NOT "BECAUSE"

Jesus explained that God does, indeed, desire our worship—but it must be "in spirit and in truth" (John 4:23–24). Affectations and embellishments, whether in physical adornments, props, or ceremonies, appeal to the flesh and, far from enhancing worship, deny both the truth and the Spirit by which it alone can be offered to the God who created and redeemed us. Sacramentalism—the belief that liturgy's form and formulas transmit spiritual power and that salvation comes through the sacraments—too readily creeps into even Protestant thinking.

Every place of worship that has been adorned for the purpose of hallowing it or gaining God's favor or making worship more acceptable violates...Scripture.

In fact, some still believe that baptism saves and that taking the bread and cup brings or sustains life.

Alas, we are all Eve's children by nature and still prone to follow the ways of Cain and the tower of Babel. Every place of worship that has been adorned for the purpose of hallowing it or gaining God's favor or making worship more acceptable violates Exodus 20:24-26 as well as the rest of Scripture. All such "sanctuaries" are monuments to man's rebellion and his proud and perverted religion of self-effort.

Billions continue, in the spirit of Babel, to pursue equally futile self-oriented religious programs to earn their way to heaven.

Unfortunately, it is all too easy to fall into the error of imagining that belonging to a church and periodically "worshiping" in its "sanctuary" makes one a Christian and compensates for one's lack of consistent, personal holiness.

Of course, no one in today's world is under the illusion that one can climb a physical tower to heaven. Yet the folly of today's religions is every bit as monumental, and the anarchy against God that motivates those beliefs is just as evil as was the Tower of Babel. Billions continue, in the spirit of Babel, to pursue equally futile self-oriented religious programs to earn their way to heaven. In the process, *truth* and *doctrine* are relegated to a secondary role, or none.

PERVERTING SAVING FAITH

Sadly, for many, faith is a power of the mind and God is merely a placebo that helps one "believe" and thereby activates this mind power. "Prayer is communicating with the deep unconscious.... Your unconscious mind... [has a] power that turns wishes into realities," said a popular Protestant leader before his recent decease. He said further, "You don't know the power you have within you!... You make the world into anything you choose." It is Babel again in a more sophisticated form. The power of "thinking" becomes the magic stairway that leads to the paradise where all one's wishes can be fulfilled.

For many Christians, the power of belief becomes one's Tower of Babel, the magic steps by which one climbs to that "state of mind called heaven."

God has blasphemously been called "the greatest Positive Thinker [or Possiblity Thinker] that ever was!" To some "faith teachers," faith is a mind power that even God uses—a force contained in words that is released when one speaks forth "the word of faith." "By the spoken word," declares the founder and pastor of the world's largest church, "we create our universe...you create the presence of Jesus with your mouth...through visualization and dreaming you can incubate your future and hatch the results." Here we have an evangelical form of Christian Science or Science of Mind. It is an abomination to the true God of the Bible.

For many Christians, the power of belief becomes one's Tower of Babel, the magic steps by which one climbs to that "state of mind called heaven." Biblical faith, however, is believing that *God* will answer one's prayer. That changes everything! We could never truly believe that a prayer would be answered—nor should we want it to be—unless we were certain it was God's will. Faith is not a magic power we direct at God to get Him to bless our plans, but "the obedience of faith" (Romans 16:26) brings us into submission to Him as the instruments of His will.

SCIENCE AS RELIGION

Humanists also have their Babel-like, do-it-yourself-kit religion. They call it science. It, too, reflects man's continued rebellion. Modern man hopes to conquer the atom, space, and all disease and thus become immortal master of the universe. The materialist's "heaven" is a peaceful cosmos populated by highly evolved, space-traveling civilizations that have restored paradise through super technology.

Rank materialism leaves the soul empty, but adding a touch of religion to science seems to fill the void...There is no more deadly delusion than a scientific religion.

Rank materialism leaves the soul empty, but adding a touch of religion to science seems to fill the void while keeping faith "rational." There is no more deadly delusion than a scientific religion. It is the delusion of Babel all over again, with advancing knowledge building the steps that both lead man to "heaven" and open to him the very powers of God.

One of Christian psychology's major appeals to evangelicals is its false claim to being scientific. It fails, however, the litmus test of Exodus 20:24-26. Its altars are built of the cut and polished stones of human wisdom, its rituals are not found in Scripture, and self rather than God is the ruler. Moreover, on its altars burn the strange fires (Leviticus 10:1; Numbers 3:4) of humanistic theories unacceptable to man's Creator.

Religious science is a major element in the environmental movement, where the earth is increasingly viewed as sacred.

Religious science is a major element in the environmental movement, where the earth is increasingly viewed as sacred. Ecotheology, says a Georgetown University professor, "starts with the premise that the Universe is God." "If we must worship a power greater than ourselves," was Carl Sagan's advice at the height of his popularity, "does it not make sense to revere the Sun and stars?" No, it does not make sense for personal beings to revere impersonal things. They ought rather to worship their Creator. To draw closer to and thus better observe and worship the heavenly bodies was a major purpose of the Tower of Babel. Worshiping "Mother Earth" is the same folly and rebellion against the true God.

The environmental movement, too, is a humanistic attempt to restore the lost paradise of Eden without repenting of rebellion against the Creator. Concern for "endangered species" by those who believe in "natural selection/survival of the fittest" is an obvious contradiction. Only those stubbornly determined to remain atheists could persist in defending evolution, which works by wiping out weaker species, and at the same time express concern for endangered species, a concern that evolution itself rejects.

BABEL'S REBELLION CONTINUES

Yet this stubborn denial of our Creator is being seductively presented in many forms to America's children in the public schools. New Age doctrine, a deadly religion, is being purposefully promoted as "culture" and even "science" in the public schools through such programs as *America 2000.*

Bill Clinton initiated school reform...at the "Governor's school"...designed to strip students of biblical morals.

As governor of Arkansas, Bill Clinton initiated school reform that had much to do with remolding the students into planetary citizens alienated from parents. Former students at the "Governor's school" testify that foul language was encouraged as part of a brainwashing procedure designed to strip students of biblical morals. There was blatant promotion of gay lifestyles, free sex, rebellion, and New Age beliefs and practices, including the worship of self and of the universe as God.

Exodus 20:24-26 is a foundational passage that makes it clear that the earth is neither to be honored nor worshiped, but to be used as an altar. Sin brought a curse upon the earth, a curse that could be removed only through the shedding of blood (Leviticus 17:11). Animals were sacrificed upon an altar of earth in anticipation of the Lamb of God, who would, "by the sacrifice of himself" (Hebrews 9:26), once and for all obtain "eternal redemption for us" (verse 12). This theme is consistently presented as the Bible's foundational doctrine from Genesis to Revelation.

It is for man's own good that God visits sin with death. How horrible it would be for mankind to continue forever in its state of rebellion, thus perpetuating ever-increasing evil, sickness, suffering, sorrow, and death. Only out of death in payment of the full penalty for sin comes resurrection (not reincarnation's amoral recycling of evil) and a whole new universe into which sin and suffering can never enter.

It is for man's own good that God visits sin with death. How horrible it would be for mankind to continue forever in its state of rebellion, thus perpetuating ever-increasing evil, sickness, suffering, sorrow, and death. Only out of death in payment of the full penalty for sin comes resurrection (not reincarnation's amoral recycling of evil) and a whole new universe into which sin and suffering can never enter.

Such is God's desire and provision for all mankind. Those who reject the free gift of eternal life offered by His grace will experience eternal regret in the tormenting finality of their endless separation from God.

The "gospel of God," as we have seen, is very specific and must be believed for one to be saved. "Strait is the gate, and narrow is the way, which leadeth unto life, and few there be that find it" (Matthew 7:14). That "narrow-minded" statement was not the invention of some dogmatic fundamentalist. It came from our Lord Jesus Christ himself.

"The faith" for which we must "earnestly contend" (Jude 3) has definite moral and doctrinal content and must be believed for salvation. All else is Babel.

11

THE CALL *to* DISCIPLESHIP

Go ye therefore, and [make disciples of] all nations...teaching them to observe all things whatsoever I have commanded you: and, lo, I am with you alway, even unto the end of the world.

—MATTHEW 28:19–20

WE SEE FROM GOD'S WORD that lost sinners are offered forgiveness of all sins (past, present, and future) and eternal life as a free gift of God's grace by virtue of Christ's fully accomplished redemptive work upon the cross and His bodily resurrection. To receive these priceless gifts, one need only believe the gospel: that one is a sinner deserving God's judgment and unable by self-effort, religious ritual, or any other means to earn or merit salvation even in part; and that Christ paid the full debt that God's justice demands for man's sin. Of course, one must believe the gospel not merely as historic fact but to the extent of placing one's faith completely in the Lord Jesus Christ as personal Savior for eternity.

Christ directed His disciples to preach the good news of the gospel to everyone everywhere. This command to His original followers has become known as the "Great Commission." It is stated in two ways: "Go ye into all the world, and *preach the gospel"* (Mark 16:15); and *"make disciples"* (Matthew 28:19–20 NASB). Those who preach the gospel are to disciple those who believe it. Born again by God's Spirit into His family (John 3:3-5; 1 John 3:2), converts begin a new life as Christ's followers, eager to learn of Him and to obey the One to whom they now owe an infinite debt of gratitude.

Faith Must Be Founded on Truth

Christ warned that some would seem to receive the gospel with great enthusiasm only to become entangled in the world, discouraged, and disillusioned. They would eventually turn back from following Him. Many maintain a façade of Christianity without inward reality, deceiving perhaps even themselves. Never fully convinced in their hearts, they are unwilling nevertheless to admit their unbelief. "Examine yourselves," Paul warned, "whether ye be in the faith" (2 Corinthians 13:5).

Of those who are genuine, all too few are able to give a reason for the hope that is in them (1 Peter 3: 15). How many Christians are able to convincingly persuade an atheist, Buddhist, Hindu, Muslim, or New Ager, with overwhelming evidence and sound reason from Scripture? God's Word is the sword of the Spirit, but few know it well enough to quell their own doubts, much less to convert others.

God's Word is the sword of the Spirit, but few know it well enough to quell their own doubts, much less to convert others.

One of today's greatest needs is for solid Bible teaching that produces disciples who are able to "earnestly contend for the faith once [for all] delivered to the saints" (Jude 3). That faith for which we must contend was delivered by Christ to the original twelve disciples, who were then to teach those whom they evangelized "*to observe all things*" that Christ had commanded them.

Through succeeding generations (beginning with the original disciples and those whom they brought to faith in Christ and discipled) of those who have been won to Him and who have in turn, in obedience to their Lord, discipled others, this unbroken chain of command comes down to us in our time. Not some special priest or clergy class, but each Christian today, like those who have passed before, is a successor to the apostles. Think of what that means!

DAILY DEATH AND RESURRECTION

At the heart of Christ's call to discipleship is the daily application of His cross in the believer's life. Yet one seldom hears in evangelical circles Christ's definitive declaration: "And whosoever doth not bear his cross, and come after me…[and] forsaketh not all that he hath, he cannot be my disciple" (Luke 14:27-33). The call to discipleship must be honestly faced. Through the cross we die to self and begin to live to our Lord in resurrection power (Galatians 2:20). Indeed, Christ's death on the cross would have been a hollow act if it did not bring forth new life, for now and for eternity.

Instead of the popular self-esteem, God calls us to deny self, to love truth and hate folly…

Resurrection life reckons the old life dead and makes no provision for the flesh (Romans 6:4,11; 13:14). Instead of the popular self-esteem, God calls us to deny self, to love truth and hate folly, to please God instead of others or ourselves—no matter what the cost in this life. Never mind social pressures from what others think, say, or do. We must be fully persuaded that what God thinks and what He will say when we appear before Him one day is all that matters.

As Jim Elliot, one of the five martyrs killed in Ecuador in 1956, said when as a young man he chose the mission field over more popular careers, "He is no fool who gives up what he cannot keep to gain what he cannot lose."

That choice is only logical if one believes that time is short and eternity is endless. Such commitment brings heavenly joy, peace, and a fulfillment that nothing earth offers can rival.

FOLLOWERS OF CHRIST

To those whom He called into a saving relationship with Himself, Christ said, "Follow me" (Matthew 4:19; 8:22; 9:9; 16:24). This simple command, which our Lord repeated after His resurrection (John 21:19,22), is as applicable to Christians today as it was when He called the first disciples.

What does it mean to follow Christ? Did He promise His followers that they would be successful, wealthy, and esteemed in this world?

God may grant earthly success to a few for His own purposes. On the whole, however, our Lord declared that those who were true to Him would follow in His path of rejection and suffering...

God may grant earthly success to a few for His own purposes. On the whole, however, our Lord declared that those who were true to Him would follow in His path of rejection and suffering: "If the world hate you, ye know that it hated me before it hated you.... The servant is not greater than his lord. If they have persecuted me, they will also persecute you...for my name's sake" (John 15:18-21).

Such was the lot of the early church. Yet today Christianity is popularized as the key to "the good life." We try to attract youth to Christ by persuading them that it's "cool" to be a Christian. The idea of suffering for Christ doesn't suit a worldly church. How strange such verses as the following seem to Christians in America: "For unto you it is given in the behalf of Christ, not only to believe on him, but also to suffer for his sake" (Philippians 1:29). Suffering is *given* to us? Paul speaks as though it were a precious privilege to suffer for His sake! After being imprisoned and beaten, the early disciples rejoiced "that they were counted worthy to suffer shame for his name" (Acts 5: 41). Such is the commitment to which the gospel actually calls us.

Today's popularized "Christianity" is further from Him and His truth than most of those who call themselves "Christian" realize.

Christ told His disciples after His resurrection, "As my Father hath sent me, even so send I you" (John 20:21). The Father sent the Son as a lamb to the slaughter into a world that would hate and crucify Him. And as the Father sent Him, so Christ sends us into a world that He promises will treat His followers as it did Him. Are we willing? Is this your idea of Christianity? If not, then think again and check it out against the Scriptures. Today's popularized "Christianity" is further from Him and His truth than most of those who call themselves "Christian" realize.

ARE WE WILLING?

Peter, who failed so miserably and was restored by the Lord, explained that true Christians would be hated, falsely accused, and persecuted, and were expected to suffer these wrongs patiently (1 Peter 2:19–20; 4:12-19). Under the inspiration of the Holy Spirit he wrote,

> For even hereunto were ye called: because Christ also suffered for us, leaving us an example, that ye should follow his steps: who did no sin, neither was guile found in his mouth: who, when he was reviled, reviled not again; when he suffered, he threatened not; but committed himself to him that judgeth righteously: who his own self bare our sins in his own body on the tree, that we, being dead to sins, should live unto righteousness.... (1 Peter 2:21-25)

Christians are being imprisoned, cruelly tortured, and martyred again in communist China, Burma, India, Indonesia, Nigeria, Sudan, and in other Muslim countries. Similar persecutions could well overtake us in America.

Recently, I listened with tears welling in my eyes as my wife, Ruth, read to me some of the history of her ancestors. For being rebaptized after they became Christians (and thus denying the efficacy of Rome's infant baptism, which many of today's Calvinists, like John Calvin himself, still practice and honor), many of these Anabaptists were drowned or burned at the stake. To escape the flames, many others fled from the Inquisition in Holland to Prussia. From there they fled to Russia, and in the closing days of World War II, many attempted an escape from godless and oppressive communism back to the West.

Out of one group of 611 leaving Russia in an attempt to return to Holland, only 31 were successful. Tramping day and night through the snow, unable to find food or shelter, some were caught and returned. Others were killed or died of exposure. Children were torn from parents, husbands from wives. The terror and agony were beyond imagination. Yet those who survived came through with their faith not only intact but strengthened.

...Thousands of Christian psychologists...make a living by encouraging their clients to pity themselves...

As Ruth read of the indescribable suffering, I thought of the thousands of Christians in America who find it necessary to enter "therapy" and spend months, if not years, dealing with comparatively trifling "hurts from the past." I thought of the thousands of Christian psychologists who make a living by encouraging their clients to pity themselves for suffering "rejection," and to pamper their "inner child," when what they need is to deny self, take up the cross, and follow Christ.

In contrast, I was inspired by the testimony of those who suffered the loss of possessions, of loved ones, of almost every earthly hope and joy, yet triumphed through their faith in Christ. Going to a "therapist" and engaging in self-pity would have seemed incomprehensible to them when they had the Lord and His Word. They knew that "our light affliction, which is but for a moment, worketh for us a far more exceeding and eternal weight of glory" (2 Corinthians 4:17).

GOD WILL BRING YOU THROUGH

Whence comes the strength to stand against overwhelming opposition and suffering and to triumph as Christ's faithful disciples? Oddly enough, victory comes not through our strength but through our weakness.

When Paul cried out for deliverance from a severe trial, Christ replied that He had allowed that suffering in order to make Paul weak enough so that he would trust only in the Lord, rather than in his great abilities. "My strength is made perfect in [your] weakness," our Lord promised (2 Corinthians 12:9).

Paul exhorts us, "As ye have therefore received Christ Jesus the Lord, so walk ye in him" (Colossians 2:6). Did we not receive Christ in weakness as helpless, hopeless sinners crying out to Him for mercy and grace? That, then, is the way we are to walk this path of triumph in suffering—as sinners saved by grace, weak and helpless in ourselves and trusting totally in Him.

We are earthen vessels, but we contain a great treasure: "that the excellency of the power may be of God, and not of us" (2 Corinthians 4:7). Such is the secret of our triumph over the world, the flesh, and the devil. The load is too heavy for us to carry. What a relief to turn it over to Him! And what a joy to be delivered from the fear of man, from seeking to win the acclaim of this world, from seeking anything but His "Well done, thou good and faithful servant" (Matthew 25:21) in that coming day.

Before God can do much *through* you, He must do a great work *in* you.

Some manage to amass a fortune to leave to their heirs at death. They seemingly forget that no hearse has a U-Haul trailer attached. Others have little of this earth's goods but have great and eternal riches laid up in heaven. It takes little wisdom to know who has made the wisest choice and who has been truly successful.

TAKING AN ETERNAL PERSPECTIVE

God has an eternal purpose for our lives now and in the life we enter after death. Our passion should be to know and to fulfill that purpose, beginning here on this earth. One day very soon we will each stand before Him. What a tragedy to miss the very purpose for which we were created and redeemed!

You may say, "Yes, I want to be used of God, but I don't know what He wants me to do." Or, "I try to serve Him, try to witness for Him, and it all seems to come to nothing."

Learn this: Before God can do much *through* you, He must do a great work *in* you. What counts most is not quantity but quality, not so much your outward effort but your motive within—the purity of your heart rather than your visible accomplishments or prominence with men.

Moreover, what seems much in time may be very little in eternity. It is not one's talents or energy but the empowering of the Holy Spirit that produces genuine and lasting results: "Not by might, nor by power, but by my spirit, saith the LORD of hosts" (Zechariah 4:6). Trust God for the filling and empowering of His Spirit.

Millions have laid down their lives for the faith. Their commitment to Christ meant so much that they would not compromise when threatened with the most excruciating torture and death. Can we fathom and follow their choice?

The martyrs could have chosen the ecumenical path of compromise, of avoiding controversy and affirming the "common beliefs of all religions," and thus have escaped the flame, drowning, or sword. They chose instead to stand firm for the truth, to contend earnestly for the faith. Christ calls us to do the same. Will we answer the call?

Paul said he had been "put in trust with the gospel" (1 Thessalonians 2:4). So have each of us if we are truly Christ's own. Let us be certain that we keep that trust for the sake of the lost and in honor of our Lord, who paid such a price for our redemption!

There is no escaping the eternal choice that confronts us. Will we follow from afar, or will we seek to follow in our Lord's very footsteps? One day we will give an account before God for the path we chose. What joy there is now and will be eternally in being true to Him.

And this is life eternal, that they might know thee the only true God, and Jesus Christ, whom thou has sent.

—JOHN 17:3

The historical and scientific evidence for the authenticity of Scripture and the true faith in Christ can be clearly seen, as demonstrated by the material in this list of recommended resources. Investigate these titles at your local library or bookstore, or see the last page of this book for details on how to order from The Berean Call.

BOOKS ON CREATION & EVOLUTION

APE MEN: FACT OR FALLACY? A CRITICAL EXAMINATION OF THE EVIDENCE
Malcom Bowden

Did you know that current theories regarding the so-called evolution of mankind are based upon inadequate fossil evidence, contrived hoaxes, and questionable discoveries? *Ape Men* demonstrates how the scientific establishment suppressed publication of evidence that would disprove their theories of human origin.

TBC# B00016

BODY BY DESIGN: THE ANATOMY & PHYSIOLOGY OF THE HUMAN BODY
Alan L. Gillen

Highlights the interwoven complexity between each of the 11 body systems, citing evidence for theistic design of specific organs and structures. Challenges readers to think through the evidence—the facts as we know them today—and to consider the statistical unlikelihood of macroevolution.

TBC# B02965

BURIED ALIVE—*Jack Cuozzo*
Neanderthal man: product of evolution? Groundbreaking research says no.

TBC# B02388

DARWIN'S BLACK BOX—*Michael J. Behe*
Was Darwin wrong? "Michael Behe has done a top-notch job of explaining and illuminating one of the most vexing problems in biology: the origin of the complexity that permeates all of life on this planet.... This book should be on the essential reading list of all those who are interested in the question of where we came from..." —Robert Shapiro

TBC# B52500

FOOTPRINTS IN THE ASH—*John Morris & Steven Austin*
Shows how the May 18, 1980 eruption of Mount Saint Helens recreated the catastrophic processes of old that may have carved out such geologic wonders as the Grand Canyon.

TBC# B03203

FOSSILS: FACTS & FANTASIES—*Joe Taylor*
The most unique book on field paleontology by the most active and knowledgeable creation paleontologist. Includes 300 color photos of some of the greatest fossil finds in the world.

TBC# B97500

HOW LIFE BEGAN—*Thomas Heinze*
With simplicity and brevity, this book presents a deluge of accurate, faith-building scientific facts. The case for intelligent design is well documented, relevant, and easy to read.

TBC# B97797

IN SIX DAYS—*John Ashton*
Can any scientist with a Ph.D. believe in a literal six-day creation? In this book, 50 scientists from around the world say yes! They answer important questions about the Big Bang Theory, radioactive dating, light from distant stars, and more.

TBC# B04432

IN THE BEGINNING—*Walt Brown, Ph.D.*
An overview of the scientific evidence for creation, including the hydroplate theory. Brown documents that the theory of a young earth is not contradicted by time concerns for the travel of light from distant galaxies.

TBC# B26011

MANY INFALLIBLE PROOFS—*Henry Morris, Ph.D.*
This resource examines the internal and external evidences for the divine nature of Scripture. Christians will be strengthened with these topics: problems in verbal inspiration, fulfillment of prophecy, the structure of Scripture, and alleged Bible contradictions.

TBC# B00059

ONE BLOOD—*Ken Ham, Carl Wieland & Don Batten*
The battle of ethnic hatred and violence remains one of the burning issues of our time. But where does the concept of "race" come from, and what does the Bible have to say?

TBC# B02760

TORNADO IN A JUNKYARD—*James Perloff*
"From molecules to man in billions of years" is the purported explanation for life and the existence of the universe. But with today's electron microscopes, DNA, and all the discoveries related to intelligent design, *Tornado in a Junkyard* takes the spin out of evolution and untwists the truth of scientific fact.

TBC# B01005

Refuting Evolution 2—*Jonathan Sarfati*
Many of the most powerful arguments in the pro-evolution crusade come from PBS-TV and the journal "Scientific American." Their three basic claims are: evolution is science, evolution is well supported by the evidence, and problems with evolution are illusory. The arguments that fall under these claims are presented and refuted.

TBC# B03365

Unlocking the Mysteries of Creation—*Dennis Petersen*
A mini-encyclopedia with color illustrations on every page! Presents a broad overview of the evidence for creation, with the Bible serving as our guide. Topics covered include UFOs, ancient civilizations, dinosaurs, and the age of the earth.

TBC# 13716

The Wonders of God—*William MacDonald*
The works of the Lord are wonderful beyond description. Everything that He has created is a marvel. A single cell is as amazing in its order and complexity as the starry heavens. The author presents an array of evidence that God is the most wonderful Person in the universe. Know Him better and love Him through the true-life drama all around you.

TBC# B00259

Video Productions

A Question of Origins—*Eternal Productions*
A fascinating presentation of the scientific evidence for special creation.

VHS • TBC# VT035 / DVD • DVD035

Dating Fossils & Rocks—*Mike Riddle*
Carbon-14 and Radioisotope dating methods—are they reliable? What are the underlying assumptions? These issues are addressed in a very clear and easy-to-understand presentation. Mike Riddle is an active adjunct professor at the Institute for Creation Research and teaches at their graduate school.

DVD • TBC# DVD061 / VHS • TBC# VT061

Science, Creation & The Bible—*American Portrait Films*
Former evolutionist Dr. Walt Brown shows the enormity of God by exploring the immensity of His creation. Your concept of God will grow as you consider the vastness of the universe and the intricacies of a single cell. Includes an easy-to-understand explanation of the hydroplate theory with helpful visuals.

TBC# VT066

INCREDIBLE CREATURES THAT DEFY EVOLUTION, VOL. 1—*Exploration Films*
Dr. Jobe Martin was a traditional evolutionist, but his medical and scientific training would go through an evolution, or rather a revolution, when he began to study animals that challenged the scientific assumptions of his education. Powerful evidence in this video proves that specialized animal designs can only be attributed to a Creator; they cannot possibly be explained by evolution.

DVD • TBC# DVD049 / VHS • TBC # VT049

INCREDIBLE CREATURES THAT DEFY EVOLUTION, VOL. 2
Exploration Films

More incredible creatures that defy evolution. The section on whales is amazing. Dr. Martin does it again!

DVD • TBC# DVD065 / VHS • TBC #VT065

UNLOCKING THE MYSTERY OF LIFE—*Illustra Media*
Using state-of-the-art computer animation, this amazing video program transports you into the interior of the living cell to explore systems and machines that bear the unmistakable hallmarks of design.

DVD • TBC# DVD056 / VHS • TBC #VT056

For the invisible things of him from
the creation of the world are clearly seen,
being understood by the things that are made,
even his eternal power and Godhead;
so that they are without excuse.

—ROMANS 1:20

The God Makers
—Ed Decker & Dave Hunt

Mormons claim to follow the same God and the same Jesus as Christians. They also state that their gospel comes from the Bible. But are they telling the truth? One of the most powerful books to penetrate the veil of secrecy surrounding the rituals and doctrines of the Mormon Church, this eye-opening exposé has been updated to reveal the current inner workings and beliefs of Mormonism. Harvest House Publishers, 292 pages.

ISBN: 1-56507-717-2 • TBC #B04023

Death of a Guru:
a remarkable true story of one man's search for truth
—Rabi R. Maharaj with Dave Hunt

Rabi R. Maharaj was descended from a long line of Brahmin priests and gurus and trained as a Yogi. He meditated for many hours each day, but gradually disillusionment set in. He describes vividly and honestly Hindu life and customs, tracing his difficult search for meaning and his struggle to choose between Hinduism and Christ. At a time when eastern mysticism, religion and philosophy fascinate many in the West, Maharaj offers fresh and important insights from the perspective of his own experience. Harvest House Publishers, 208 pages.

ISBN: 0-89081-434-1 • TBC #B04341

The Seduction of Christianity:
spiritual discernment in the last days
—Dave Hunt & Tom McMahon

The Bible clearly states that a great Apostasy must occur before Christ's Second Coming. Today Christians are being deceived by a new world view more subtle and more seductive than anything the world has ever experienced. Scripture declares that this seduction will not appear as a frontal assault or oppression of our religious beliefs; instead, it will come as the latest "fashionable philosophies" offering to make us happier, healthier, better educated, even more spiritual. As the first bestselling book to sound the alarm of false teaching in the church, this ground-breaking classic volume still sounds a clear call to every believer to choose between the Original and the counterfeit. As delusions and deceptions continue to grow, this book will guide you in the truth of God's Word. Harvest House Publishers, 239 pages.

ISBN: 0-89081-441-4 • TBC #B04414

IN DEFENSE OF THE FAITH: BIBLICAL ANSWERS TO CHALLENGING QUESTIONS
—Dave Hunt

Why does God allow suffering and evil? What about all the "contradictions" in the Bible? Are some people predestined to go to hell? This book tackles the tough issues that Christians and non-Christians alike wonder about today, including why a merciful God would punish people who have never heard of Christ, how to answer attacks against God's existence and the Bible, and how to tell the difference between God's workings and Satan's. Harvest House, 347 pages.

ISBN: 1-56507-495-5 • TBC #B04955

THE NONNEGOTIABLE GOSPEL
—Dave Hunt

A must for the Berean soul-winner's repertory, this evangelistic booklet reveals the gem of the gospel in every clear-cut facet. Refines and condenses what Dave has written for believers to use as a witnessing tool for anyone desiring a precise Bible definition of the gospel. The Berean Call, 48 pages.

ISBN: 1-928660-01-0 • TBC #B45645

BATTLE FOR THE MIND
–Dave Hunt

Positive thinking is usually better than negative thinking and can sometimes help a great deal, but it has its limitations. To deny those commonsense limitations and to believe that the mind can create its own universe is to step into the occult where the demons who foster this belief will eventually destroy the soul. Unfortunately, increasing millions in the West are accepting this mystical philosophy, forgetting that it is the very thing which has brought many deplorable conditions wherever it has been practiced. The Berean Call, 48 pages.

ISBN: 1-928660-09-6 • TBC #B45650

DEBATING CALVINISM: FIVE POINTS, TWO VIEWS
—Dave Hunt & James White

Is God free to love anyone He wants? Do you have any choice in your own salvation? "This book deserves to be read carefully by anyone interested in the true nature of God." —Tim LaHaye, co-author of the Left Behind series. Calvinism has been a topic of intense discussion for centuries. In this lively debate, two passionate thinkers take opposite sides, providing valuable responses to the most frequently asked questions about Calvinism. Only you can decide where you stand on questions that determine how you think about your salvation.

ISBN: 1-590522-73-7 • TBC #B05000

When Will Jesus Come?
COMPELLING EVIDENCE FOR THE SOON RETURN OF CHRIST
—Dave Hunt

Jesus has promised to return for His bride, the church. But when will that be? In this updated revision of How Close Are We?, Dave takes us on a journey through the Old and New Testaments as he explains prophecy after prophecy showing that we are indeed in the last of the last days. In the process, Dave compellingly shows that Scripture illuminates the truth that Jesus will return two times, and that His next appearance—the "rapture" of His church—will occur without any warning. The question is, are you ready? Harvest House Publishers, 251 pages.

ISBN: 0-7369-1248-7 • TBC #B03137

Countdown to the Second Coming:
A CHRONOLOGY OF PROPHETIC EARTH EVENTS HAPPENING NOW
—Dave Hunt

At last, a book that presents in a concise manner the events leading up to the return of Christ. Dave Hunt, in his characteristic direct style, answers questions such as, Who is the Antichrist? How will he be recognized? How are current events indicators that we really are in the last of the last days? Using Scripture and up-to-date information, Dave draws the exciting conclusion that, indeed, time is short. He helps you to realize what your response should be and then reminds you of the hope that you have in the gospel. This book instructs, encourages, warns, and strengthens, urging readers to "walk circumspectly, not as fools, but as wise, redeeming the time, because the days are evil" (Ephesians 5:15-16). The Berean Call, new paperback edition, 96 pages.

ISBN: 1-928660-19-3

A Woman Rides the Beast:
The Roman Catholic Church and the Last Days
—Dave Hunt

In Revelation 17, the Apostle John describes in great detail the characteristics of a false church that will be the partner of the Antichrist. Was he describing the Roman Catholic Church? To answer that question, Dave has spent years gathering research and indisputable historical documentation (primarily Catholic sources) providing information not generally available. Harvest House, 549 pages.

ISBN: 1-56507-199-9 • TBC #B01999

Occult Invasion:
THE SUBTLE SEDUCTION OF THE WORLD AND CHURCH
—Dave Hunt

Occult beliefs march freely across America today powerfully influencing our children, our society, our government, and even out churches. The deadly impact of Satan's dominion is seen in the rise of teen suicide, the increase in violence, and the immorality that pervades our society. Sharing the knowledge you need to protect your family from this invasion, noted cult expert Dave Hunt reveals: how Satan's lies are being taught behind the academic respectability of science; how demonic activities are presented as the path to enlightenment through "alien" contacts and paranormal experiences; how pagan religions are being promoted through ecology and "we are one" philosophies; and how evil is being reinvented as good by psychology and the legal system. This powerful volume gives you the skills you need to recognize the subtle incursions of the occult and provides tools you can use to protect your family, church, and all who will listen from its destructive advance. Harvest House Publishers, 647 pages.

ISBN: 1-56507-269-3 • TBC #B02693

What Love is This?
CALVINISM'S MISREPRESENTATION OF GOD
—Dave Hunt

It takes only a few simple questions to discover the fact that most of those who regard themselves as Calvinists are largely unaware of what John Calvin and his early followers of the sixteenth and seventeenth centuries actually believed and practiced. Nor do they fully understand what most of today's leading Calvinists believe. While there are disputed variations of this doctrine, among its cheif proponents (whom we quote extensively in context) there is general agreement on certain core beliefs. Multitudes who believe they understand Calvinism will be shocked to discover its Roman Catholic roots and Calvin's grossly un-Christian behavior as the "Protestant Pope" of Geneva, Switzerland. Most shocking of all, however, Calvinism's misrepresentation of God who "is love." It is our prayer that this book will enable readers to examine more carefully the vital issues involved and to follow God's Holy Word and not man. The Berean Call, 576 pages.

ISBN: 1-928660-12-6 • TBC #B03000

About The Berean Call

The Berean Call (TBC) is a nonprofit,
tax-exempt corporation which exists to:

ALERT believers in Christ to unbiblical teachings and practices impacting the church

EXHORT believers to give greater heed to biblical discernment and truth regarding teachings and practices being currently promoted in the church

SUPPLY believers with teaching, information, and materials which will encourage the love of God's truth, and assist in the development of biblical discernment

MOBILIZE believers in Christ to action in obedience to the scriptural command to "earnestly contend for the faith" (Jude 3)

IMPACT the church of Jesus Christ with the necessity for trusting the Scriptures as the only rule for faith, practice, and a life pleasing to God

---

A free monthly newsletter, The Berean Call, *may be received by sending a request to: PO Box 7019, Bend, OR 97708; or by calling*

1-800-937-6638

To register for free email updates, to access our digital archives, and to order a variety of additional resource materials online, visit us at:

WWW.THEBEREANCALL.ORG

Bend • Oregon